THE GUARANTEED CUSTOMER EXPERIENCE

How to Win Customers by Keeping Your Promises

JEFF TOISTER

ISBN 978-0-578-82494-9

Book design: Anne C. Kerns, Anne Likes Red, Inc.

THE GUARANTEED
CUSTOMER EXPERIENCE

JeffToister
Your Service Culture Guide

Thanks for joining
me on the
Yelp webinar!

—Jeff

ACKNOWLEDGEMENTS

Thank you to Denise Lee Yohn for convincing me to move forward with this book. And thank you to Leslie O'Flahavan for helping me get unstuck when the book wasn't moving forward.

I admire you both and truly appreciate your support, friendship, and wise counsel.

CONTENTS

START HERE

Life was tough for customers in the mid-1800s.

Consumers in the United States had few protections against fraud. Companies took advantage of this, making all sorts of unverifiable claims to market and sell their products. There was little a customer could do if those claims were exaggerated or false. This was especially true in rural areas, where competitors were few and customers had limited options for purchasing essential items.

One field especially rife with fraud was patent medicine. These unprescribed elixirs, tonics, and liniments were marketed as "miracle cures" for various ailments and pains. Patent medicines sold in the mid-1800s often failed to work, and many contained dangerous amounts of opium or other narcotics.

Nonetheless, these products were aggressively promoted. Companies selling patent medicines created many modern-day advertising tactics, such as direct mail, free samples, promotional items with purchase, and testimonials from purportedly satisfied customers.[1]

In 1868, an entrepreneur named Joseph Ray Watkins created his own patent medicine, a pain relief liniment that he sold door-to-door in rural Minnesota. The active ingredient was camphor from evergreen trees rather than dangerous opioids, and the product worked well. Watkins recognized the value of building trust and long-term relationships with customers, and in 1869, he created a novel marketing technique to stand out from the competition.

He is credited for offering the first money-back guarantee in America.

The liniment came in glass bottles that had "trial mark" and a horizontal line molded into the glass about a third of the way down from the top. Watkins promised to refund customers' money if they were unsatisfied with his liniment, as long as the contents had not been used below the trial mark line. He typically called on customers every three months, which gave him the opportunity to either make good on his guarantee or verify that he had yet another satisfied customer.[2]

The guarantee demonstrated that Watkins wasn't just interested in earning the next sale. He wanted to win customers and then keep their business over the long run. Of course, his liniment actually had to work for this plan to succeed. Otherwise, he would have lost all his profits refunding customers' money and losing out on their next purchase.

Today's landscape is more complicated for businesses than it was in the mid-1800s. There are more laws protecting consumers, and it's easier for potential customers to research a brand's reputation and reliability before making a purchase. Unsatisfied customers share their complaints online, where anyone in the world can learn about their experience. Thanks to the internet, customers have an array of choices that would have been unimaginable to consumers in the 19th century.

Many patent medicines from the 1800s are long gone, but you can still buy J.R. Watkins Pain Relieving Liniment today. It enjoys high ratings from customer reviews on Amazon, Walmart, and other merchants. And customers who buy directly from the J.R. Watkins company can still return the product for a refund if they're unsatisfied.[3]

A guarantee can be a powerful marketing tool for winning and retaining customers, but it needs to be modernized from the 1800s. People have become emotionally connected to the brands, products, and services they know and trust. They don't just want a product to work and good customer service if something goes wrong. Customers want to have a great *experience*.

What if you could guarantee customer experience?

Creating a consistently great customer experience seems like a complicated and daunting task. Customers have a wide range of ever-changing wants and needs. Consultants and academics promote a dizzying array of tools and techniques, such as customer journey mapping, customer personas, customer anthropology, social listening, sentiment analysis, and Net Promoter Scores.

It doesn't have to be that complicated.

The Guaranteed Customer Experience shows you how to take the old concept of a guarantee and modernize it for today's customer. You'll discover a simple way to guarantee that your customers will have an amazing experience—and then consistently deliver on that promise.

This book reveals how brands, products, and even individual employees can use the Guaranteed Customer Experience model to stand out from the competition. Here are a few examples of actual experience guarantees you'll learn about:

★ You will become a better gardener.

★ A new bed will be delivered before your guests arrive.

★ You will grow your business.

★ Your backpack will help you enjoy outdoor adventures.

★ The delicious pizza you ordered will arrive on time.

These guarantees seem deceptively simple at first, yet they work because they're incredibly compelling to customers—and because other companies struggle to match them.

An experience guarantee provides three primary benefits to help your business grow.

First, you will attract more new customers by promising a consistently good experience tailored to their needs.

3

Second, you'll retain existing customers by consistently delivering on that promise.

And finally, you'll create customer evangelists who will help promote your business because you consistently deliver something your customers value, and your competition just can't seem to get right.

Who should read this book?

The Guaranteed Customer Experience is intended for anyone who wants to win and retain customers by offering a consistently superior customer experience.

Company executives, whether you're a small business owner or a Fortune 500 CEO, can use this model to build a customer-focused organization. Functional leaders—such as marketing managers, product managers, and customer service managers—will discover how to build more unity and cooperation with other departments. Even individual employees will benefit by learning how to manage customer expectations and recover from service failures.

The Guaranteed Customer Experience will help whether you're just beginning to learn about customer experience as a discipline, or you're an advanced practitioner. Beginners will discover a model that's easy to implement and understand. Advanced customer experience experts will learn a critical piece that's been missing from previous customer experience initiatives.

The model works whether you're business-to-consumer, business-to-business, or in a hybrid industry. Most of the examples of experience guarantees you'll read about come from business-to-consumer companies. That's merely because those stories are relatable to the widest audience, but a few business-to-business examples are included to show how versatile this approach can be.

My guarantee to you

There are many other books that promise to help you win and retain customers. Frankly, it's easy: the author simply types the words and publishes the book. There's rarely any real accountability.

So I want to offer you a Guaranteed Customer Experience for reading this book. This guarantee becomes effective once you've completed the exercises and implemented the Guaranteed Customer Experience model detailed in the following chapters:

You will gain something from reading this book that you can use to win and retain more customers. I will give you a free one-hour phone coaching session if you implement the Guaranteed Customer Experience model and are not happy with the results.

Using the guarantee is easy. If you're unhappy with the results you achieve from implementing the Guaranteed Customer Experience model, schedule a one-hour call with me, and we'll discuss how to get better results. I won't pawn you off on an assistant or make you jump through an endless series of hoops. Simply use this link to schedule a one-hour call with me at a date and time of your convenience: guaranteedexperience.com/guarantee.

You might find yourself needing some advice or assistance while you're in the process of implementing a Guaranteed Customer Experience. Should you have any questions about the process, please feel free to contact me directly. Here is my personal contact information:

★ **Call or text**: 619-955-7946

★ **Email**: jeff@toistersolutions.com

Yes, there is a risk in making my time and contact information so readily available. I do it to demonstrate the power of the Guaranteed Customer Experience model. If I've done my job correctly by presenting a process to you that's easy to understand, follow, and implement, and the process *actually works*, then very few readers will need to collect on that guarantee or contact me for support. The ones that do need my help will likely have encountered an unexpected or challenging issue that will be a learning opportunity for both of us.

My aims are similar to yours: I hope to attract new readers, retain your readership when I publish books in the future, and earn evangelists who will tell other people about this book.

For me to achieve my goals, you need to achieve yours. So if you're ready, turn to Chapter 1, and let's get started. You'll learn about a company that attracts customers with a promise that's so mind-bogglingly simple, you'll wonder why its competitors aren't doing the same thing.

Notes

1   "Balm of America: Patent Medicine Collection," National Museum of American History website, https://americanhistory.si.edu/collections/object-groups/balm-of-america-patent-medicine-collection/history, accessed September 12, 2020.

2   Robert L. Williams, Jr. and Helena A. Williams, *Vintage Marketing Differentiation: The Origins of Marketing and Branding Strategies*, Palgrave Macmillan, New York, 2017.

3   The J.R. Watkins return policy offers refunds up to $35 within the first 30 days of purchase, https://jrwatkins.com/pages/shipping-returns, accessed September 18, 2020.

PART I

Winning Customers with Guarantees

Chapter 1

IDENTIFYING YOUR CUSTOMER'S PROBLEM

Imagine driving cross-country on a road trip.

You need gas, and you need to use the restroom. Choosing a place to stop is a big decision. Gas stations can be miles apart. The station you see on the horizon probably has gas, but there's no guarantee they'll have a clean restroom. Do you need to stop now, or do you have enough fuel to keep going until the next one?

You size up each gas station's convenience store you pass as your level of urgency increases. Some are rejected at first glance for being too scary. You slow to scrutinize others. Will the restroom be open or out-of-order? Will there be a line? Will it be clean?!

Your car's gas gauge is hovering near "E," while your own tank is dangerously close to "F." Decision time. Where will you stop?

You're not alone in this experience. A study from the travel app GasBuddy found that 40 percent of Americans worry about finding a clean restroom on a road trip.[1]

Buc-ee's, a chain of gas station convenience stores located primarily in Texas, has developed a devoted customer base by solving this problem. Driving through Texas, you're likely to encounter any number of humorous billboards advertising the nearest Buc-ee's location:

★ "Top two reasons to stop at Buc-ee's: #1 and #2."

★ "Let us plan your next potty."

★ "Restrooms so clean we leave mints in the urinals."

★ "Our aim is to have clean restrooms. Your aim will help."

★ "Your throne awaits. Fabulous restrooms."

The billboards speak clearly to customers on the go who desperately have to go. They demonstrate an understanding of this common road trip problem and promise that Buc-ee's will solve it. Many travelers will drive past other gas stations to get to a Buc-ee's, because Buc-ee's provides an assurance that other brands don't.

Your heart might skip a beat when you walk into a Buc-ee's for the first time. The restrooms are clearly visible from the front entrance, but so is the steady stream of people walking in and out of them. Will there be a long line? Or worse, will it be a mess?

Buc-ee's does not disappoint. 8.3 million ratings of fuel and convenience retailers on the GasBuddy travel app rated the restrooms at Buc-ee's as the best in America.[2] The restrooms at each location are unbelievably plentiful and clean, and each is well-stocked with paper and soap. Many are downright enormous.

The Buc-ee's in Katy, Texas, has a whopping 28 toilets in the women's room and 30 urinals and 12 toilets in the men's room. The restrooms alone are larger than a typical convenience store. There are lights above each stall that illuminate in red when the stall is occupied and green when the stall is available, which helps you avoid awkward door jiggling or shoe gazing. They're continuously patrolled by employees who keep the toilet paper and hand towels well-stocked and the restrooms sparkling.

Clean restrooms attract customers, but that's not all Buc-ee's has to offer.

It has all the items you'd expect to see in a convenience store — such as soda, candy, and chips — though on a much larger scale. The New Braunfels location, which is thought to be the world's largest convenience store at 68,000 square feet, has 80 fountain dispensers, 120 fuel pumps, and 27 cash registers.[3]

There are also things you wouldn't expect to find in a typical convenience store. Larger Buc-ee's locations have a barbecue counter where employees make hot sandwiches to order. There's an enormous display of house-made beef jerky and candy. Keep walking, and you'll come to a large section selling Texas-themed gifts and Buc-ee's apparel.

I once stopped at the Buc-ee's in Luling, Texas, to get a dog leash. My wife and I were on a road trip, and I had accidentally left our dog's leash at my mother-in-law's house in Houston. "Let's stop at Buc-ee's," I said. "I bet they have dog leashes." Sure enough, they did.

The size of the store and the sheer number of customers can intimidate first-time visitors, but Buc-ee's is surprisingly convenient. There are multiple cash register lines open with friendly cashiers ready and waiting to serve you.

Buc-ee's draws large crowds. Its locations average nearly four times as many customers as a typical convenience store.[4]

Imagine attracting four times more customers to your business than your competition. What would cause so many customers to give you a try and, once they did, keep coming back? The secret is customer experience.

What Is Customer Experience?

Customer experience and customer service often get confused with each other. It doesn't help that both companies and their customers frequently use the terms interchangeably.

The distinction is important, since customer service is just one aspect of the overall customer experience.

Annette Franz is a certified customer experience professional and consultant who helps companies become more customer-focused. Franz shared this definition of customer experience on her *CX Journey* blog: "The sum of all the interactions that a customer has with an organization over the life of the relationship with that company and, especially, the feelings, emotions, and perceptions the customer has about those interactions."[5]

A traveler's first interaction with Buc-ee's might be one of those funny billboards they see along the highway. Perhaps they see several. (I counted 19 on one stretch of highway in Texas.) The experience continues as they pull into the enormous parking lot and see row after row of gas pumps and a building many times larger than the typical convenience store. Once inside, the spotless restrooms and huge product selection are further confirmation that Buc-ee's is very different than the typical gas station.

Franz's definition of customer experience includes all interactions a customer has with a brand, even those that happen outside of a shopping experience. Let's say a customer is so enthralled with the store that they buy a Buc-ee's t-shirt. (Guilty, I have one.) Wearing that t-shirt in public is sure to garner appreciative comments from fellow Buc-ee's fans. That becomes part of the customer experience, even when the person wearing the t-shirt is hundreds of miles from the nearest Buc-ee's location.

Customer *service* is more narrowly defined than *experience*. According to the *Oxford English Dictionary*, customer service is "The assistance and advice provided by a company to those people who buy or use its products or services."[6]

This means customer service is an important part of customer experience, but it's not all of it. Examples of customer service might be a retail salesperson helping a customer select a new television, a technical support rep helping a customer troubleshoot a software program, or a stadium usher helping a group of fans find their seats.

The Buc-ee's experience includes great customer service. There are lots of friendly employees who answer questions, serve up hot sandwiches, and ring up your purchases. The experience also includes many elements that are not customer service, such as the clean restrooms or enormous product selection.

Think about the customer experience your company offers. What are some elements that aren't considered part of customer service, but which have an impact on the feelings, emotions, and perceptions customers have about your brand? Here are some examples:

★ Advertising

★ Website

★ Product packaging

★ Product delivery

★ Billing

If your business has physical locations, there are many aspects of *experience* that are not part of *service*. Where your business is located in relation to your customers determines how easy or difficult it is for customers to travel to you. The availability of parking and other transportation options are also factors. The décor, product displays, location of cash registers and employee work stations, and even the music playing in the background are all part of the customer experience.

The design of your products and the way a customer uses them are part of the experience, too. Your favorite pair of shoes is a great example. The way the shoes look, the way they make you feel when you wear them, and the way they perform when you walk in them are all part of your experience.

The quality of the products you sell is also important. Do they work as intended, or do customers struggle to use them? Are they easy for customers to assemble, or do customers get confused and return them at a high rate? Are your products reliable and top quality, or do they break prematurely?

Third-party interactions can also play a vital role in customer experience. A furniture store that relies on a separate delivery company has made that delivery company part of the furniture-buying experience. Having a third-party company provide warranty repairs or answer calls made to a customer hotline means those companies are part of the experience, too.

Consistency is another aspect of experience. Do customers have a similar experience every time they interact with your company? For companies or franchises with multiple locations, is the experience consistent no matter where a customer visits? Or do your products, service, and employee interactions vary widely?

How Experience Can Set You Apart from the Competition

Customer experience can be overwhelming. The idea that experience encompasses literally all interactions customers have with your brand makes it impossible to identify and manage every single aspect. Many executives recognize the importance of customer experience, but don't know where to start.

The good news is, your business doesn't need to serve every imaginable customer need. You can differentiate your company, department, or location from the competition by identifying one problem your customer is trying to solve, and then consistently solving that problem better than anyone else.

There are a lot of coffee shops in my neighborhood. Many have good customer service with friendly, helpful employees, but I only go to two. One is a Starbucks, which has thousands of locations around the world. The other is The Simple Coffee House, or Simple, which has just one location.

The specific coffee shop I choose depends on the problem I'm trying to solve that day.

Starbucks is better at convenience than any other coffee chain, so I go there when I need to grab a quick cup of coffee. I can pay for my drink via the Starbucks app, and I can even use the app to order ahead of time, so my drink is waiting for me when I arrive. This particular Starbucks is located near a freeway, so it's easy to stop on my way home or when I'm heading out. It doesn't have a drive-through lane, but there's always a parking spot available near the entrance, so I can get in and out quickly.

The Simple Coffee House competes with Starbucks by being a great place to meet a friend or find a place to set up my laptop and get some work done. Seating is more plentiful than at my local Starbucks, so I know my friend and I will have a comfortable place to sit and chat without feeling crowded by other guests. There are lots of power outlets spread throughout the seating area if I need to charge my phone or computer. There's a record player near the front playing old jazz records, creating a fun vibe. The coffee at Simple is much better than at Starbucks, which is important when I want to relax and enjoy my beverage.

Offering a great experience to customers like me who are looking for a place to gather allows Simple to compete with large, established coffee chains like Starbucks. Simple is less convenient than Starbucks—it's farther from the freeway, there's no way to place an order in advance, and drinks take slightly longer to make. But Simple has an excellent reputation in the neighborhood with a 4.5-star rating on Yelp.[7]

Simple's Yelp rating is due in large part to many customer experience elements that make it a great place to meet a friend or get some work done. Here are the percentage of Yelp reviews that include positive mentions of key attributes:

★ Great coffee (79 percent)

★ Inviting atmosphere (46 percent)

★ Ample seating (32 percent)

★ Vinyl record player (24 percent)

★ Plenty of power outlets (18 percent)

Consistency is an important part of customer experience. People need to know they can count on your brand. The Starbucks I go to near my house has a seating area where I could meet a friend or get some work done, but it's often crowded. There have been many occasions when all the tables were taken or no outlets were available, so I can't be sure that the Starbucks will be a good place to sit and stay on any given day.

So where does customer service fit in, and is it still important? Yes! Customer service is part of the overall experience, so it plays a critical role in attracting and retaining customers.

Simple's Yelp reviews call out great customer service 65 percent of the time. Many of those reviews mention specific people by name for making customers feel welcome.

There's another Starbucks location that's about the same distance from my home as the one I frequent. It's equally convenient, but the employees at this location are less friendly. That poor customer service causes me to choose one location over another.

Think about the choices you make as a customer. There's a good chance many of the companies you do business with do one thing really well that's important to you, even if other elements of the experience aren't perfect. You're loyal to a certain brand of shampoo because it makes your hair look fabulous, even though it's more expensive. The airline you fly upsets you with extra fees, but it has comfortable planes and offers the most direct flights from your local airport. There's often a wait at your favorite restaurant, but the food is amazing, and friendly servers call you by name and remember your favorite dish.

Buc-ee's wins customers from competing brands by consistently providing restrooms that are far superior to anyone else's. It averages a four-star rating on Yelp across all locations, with a whopping 46 percent of those reviews mentioning the restrooms.[8] Cody Esser, who writes the *Impulsive Traveler Guy* blog, traveled to 33 Buc-ee's locations over the course of three days in 2018. He reported that not a single restroom at any of those locations was dirty.[9] I polled family and friends in Texas, asking what they love about Buc-ee's. Nearly everyone mentioned the clean restrooms.

Of course, the Buc-ee's experience is more than just clean restrooms. It keeps customers coming back with stores that are bigger and have a broader selection of items than a typical gas station convenience store. My friend Robin summarized the Buc-ee's experience nicely: "I love that you can get bakery items, fresh-made candy, wonderful hot sandwiches, that they have a gift shop, and also have clean bathrooms! They have everything a traveler could ever want."

The challenge for any business is to figure out exactly what problem it can consistently solve better than the competition. It has to be something that customers value so customers choose you over other options. Creating a Guaranteed Customer Experience will help you solve this dilemma.

The Guaranteed Customer Experience Model

Amazon dominates e-commerce in many markets around the world. In the United States alone, the company is responsible for an estimated 37.3 percent of all online sales.[10] One reason people habitually buy from Amazon is it consistently solves one problem quickly and conveniently: "I need to buy _____."

You can fill in the blank with nearly every product imaginable. Customers flock to Amazon to buy books, groceries, and household goods, as well as larger items such as ping pong tables, surfboards, and furniture.

The Amazon website is easy to search across multiple product categories. Many products have hundreds or even thousands of customer reviews. Once you find something you like, you can often order it with a single click. Depending on where you live, most products can be delivered in as little as one day (sometimes faster). The company is famously reliable and uses rigorous process controls to prevent shipping errors. It's also remarkably consistent at meeting its promised delivery windows.

A study from the research firm Walker Sands discovered that 41 percent of respondents chose Amazon over other options to purchase a product because of faster delivery. Among those customers, 15 percent purchased from Amazon despite cheaper prices elsewhere.[11]

Throughout this book, you'll meet companies like Amazon and Buc-ee's that have won loyal customers by identifying the problems their customers face and then solving them consistently. These companies have built customer-focused cultures that align marketing, operations, customer service, and other departments around helping their customers succeed. This commitment to customer experience is so strong, they guarantee it.

A typical guarantee makes a promise, such as how long a product will last without breaking, or that customers will be totally satisfied with their purchase. Behind the scenes, companies must work hard to keep those promises or risk losing both credibility and customers. Guarantees often include a specific remedy in the event a promise isn't kept—such as refunding the customer's money or replacing a defective product. The remedy gives customers an extra amount of assurance and creates an additional financial incentive for companies to keep their promises.

The Guaranteed Customer Experience model applies the concept of a guarantee to the customer's overall experience. You win customers by promising to solve a customer's problem, retain customers by making sure that promise is kept, and encourage unhappy customers to give you another chance by recovering from service failures.

Identifying the problem your customer is trying to solve is at the core of the Guaranteed Customer Experience model. Once you understand your customer's problem, you can create a guarantee to solve it that ensures your customer has a great experience. We'll cover the rest of the model in future chapters.

For now, let's start by identifying a customer problem that you can solve.

Exercise: What Problem Does Your Customer Have?

This book contains a series of exercises to help you create your own Guaranteed Customer Experience. You'll find these exercises at the end of each chapter.

The goal of this first exercise is to create a one-sentence problem statement that clearly describes a common customer problem. In future chapters, you'll use this problem statement to construct an experience guarantee that wins and retains customers.

There are two steps to writing the customer problem statement. The first is to identify a customer problem. The second is to write a problem statement that describes the issue in one simple sentence.

I created a workbook to help you complete this exercise and others you'll do throughout the book. You can download it at guaranteedexperience.com/workbook.

Identify a Customer Problem

The problem you choose to focus on for this exercise depends on your role.

If you're a business owner, CEO, or senior executive, think about a fundamental problem your business solves. For example, a company selling electronic medical records software might serve hospitals and medical centers needing to efficiently track patient records.

If you're a product manager, think about a problem your product solves. A tile grout cleaner might help consumers who need to keep the tile in their kitchens and bathrooms looking new.

If you're a department manager, think about a problem your team solves. A purchasing manager might support a factory that needs to have the right raw materials on hand to build products. A contact center manager might serve customers who need to get help with a billing, delivery, or product issue.

If you're an individual contributor, think about a common problem your customers face. For instance, if you're a restaurant delivery driver, you help customers who need a convenient way to get the food they ordered delivered fresh and on time.

This is unlikely to be a new problem you've never heard about. Rather, it should be a problem you're already aware of, and this exercise will help bring clarity about how you can address it.

You can also use customer feedback to help identify a problem to solve. Many people instantly equate feedback with surveys, but you can also get feedback from direct customer conversations, listening to social media and online reviews, and even observing your customers.

Here are some questions that can help identify a customer problem:

★ What problem do your customers discuss most often?

★ What is the reason your customers choose you over other options?

★ What does your customer do with your product or service?

My recommendation is to focus on finding just one problem to start with, and use it to create your first Guaranteed Customer Experience. You can go back and create more guarantees once you successfully implement the model for the first time.

Warning: Identifying your customer's problem requires you to see your business from your customer's perspective. For instance, if you want to know what someone on a road trip wants most from a gas station convenience store, just imagine being that customer. Once you do this, the problem is often quickly revealed. There's a good chance you already know what it is.

This is not the time to convene endless committees or study groups. In my experience, this kind of corporate over-think almost always causes people to miss something obvious.

Write a Problem Statement

The second step is to write a problem statement. The statement should be written from your customer's perspective, focusing on their problem rather than your viewpoint.

Start your problem statement with the words, "I need to." Imagine what your customer would say as they describe their problem. Here are some examples:

★ Buc-ee's: "I need to use the restroom."

★ The Simple Coffee Shop: "I need to meet a friend for coffee."

★ Amazon: "I need to get something quickly."

I created a problem statement while writing this book. My goal was to identify the problem you were trying to solve when you decided to read it.

"I need to win and retain more customers."

Write your problem statement before moving on to the next chapter. Then you'll have a real-life example to work with, providing important context as we walk through the steps to create a Guaranteed Customer Experience.

Chapter 1 Notes

1   GasBuddy, "What a 'Relief'! GasBuddy Study Finds Gas Station Restrooms Are Getting Cleaner, Reveals Top Rated Restrooms In Every State for Peak Road Trip Season," news release, May 14, 2019.

2   GasBuddy, "2019 Fuel and Convenience Store Scorecard," February 11, 2020.

3   Hannah Denham, "A Texas-size mart's road to fame," *The Washington Post*, August 14, 2019.

4   GasBuddy, "2019 Fuel and Convenience Store Scorecard," February 11, 2020.

5   Annette Franz, "Customer Experience and Customer Service: What's the Difference?" *CX Journey* blog, October 3, 2018.

6   *Oxford English Dictionary*, accessed October 4, 2020, https://www.lexico.com/en/definition/customer_service.

7   Yelp reviews for The Simple Coffee House, accessed May 13, 2020, https://www.yelp.com.

8   Data provided by Yelp for January 2019-May 2020.

9   Cody Esser, "Buc-ee Mania: Hitting Up Every Buc-ee's In Texas," *Impulsive Traveler Guy* blog, June 26, 2018.

10 "Amazon Remains the Undisputed No. 1," *eMarketer*, March 11, 2020.

11 Walker Sands, "Future of Retail 2018," 2018.

Chapter 2

WHAT MAKES A GREAT GUARANTEE?

Jenny Dempsey struggled to keep her houseplants alive.

"I don't have a green thumb," she wrote on her *Customer Service Life* blog. "I over/under water and clearly just don't get it. I always think I'm doing alright, but it doesn't always show up that way in my growing, er wilting, plants."[1]

Dempsey's experience at a big box store was less than satisfying. "I used to shop at Home Depot for plants, as it was closer to my home. But after having several failed attempts at asking for help, including one where an employee told me that she 'had no clue' about where something was located in the store, then quickly walked away from me, I ditched the depot and found a new place to shop."

That new place was Armstrong Garden Centers, a chain of nurseries with more than 30 stores throughout California, and more than 15 operating under the Pike Nurseries brand in Georgia and North Carolina. She went to the location in Encinitas, California, and purchased a calathea plant. Unfortunately, the plant struggled to thrive once she brought it home.

Dempsey knew she needed help, but her experience with other brands made her hesitant. "I didn't know if I could actually walk in there with the plant," she said. So she decided to call the store.

An Armstrong associate named Kim gave her some pointers and invited Dempsey to bring her plant to the store so someone could take a closer look. She was already impressed that Kim was empowered to help her. "No one had to put me on hold to ask for a manager."

Dempsey headed for the store with her calathea. Another associate, Carrie, greeted her when she arrived. Amazingly, Carrie was expecting her and knew about her plant, having already been briefed by Kim. Carrie gave her some suggestions for reviving the calathea, and Dempsey left the store with renewed confidence in her ability to keep her houseplants alive.

She followed Carrie's suggestions and her calathea slowly recovered. "They gave me faith in my plant skills," said Dempsey, who vowed to be a loyal Armstrong customer for all her plants and plant care needs.

Expert advice from associates like Carrie and Kim makes it easier for customers like Dempsey to feel more confident. "Walking in there with basically a half-dead plant, no one made me feel stupid. No matter how much I read online, it really helps to have a place to walk in and to have people that take the time to talk to you."

Armstrong Garden Centers wins and retains customers like Dempsey by operating under a philosophy of *Gardening without Guesswork.* The company's website explains the meaning to potential job applicants. "These three little words guide all of our actions at Armstrong Garden Centers from how we engage with our customers, to the products we bring into our stores and with our operational excellence. We are here to take the guesswork out of gardening for our customers."[2]

In Chapter 1, we discussed how a great experience comes from consistently solving your customers' problems. People come to Armstrong because they want make their garden look beautiful, grow delicious vegetables, or keep their houseplants alive.

Great customer service is an important part of the *Gardening without Guesswork* experience. Helpful, friendly employees are mentioned in 70 percent of the Yelp reviews for Armstrong's

Encinitas store.[3] Employees patiently share expert advice and help customers pick the right plants. They also advise customers on the best soil, feeding regimen, and watering schedule to keep plants healthy.

Armstrong provides a lot of proactive customer service to give gardeners extra help when planning their gardens. Stores offer gardening classes and in-home landscape design services. Experts are available to give garden talks at local organizations. The Armstrong website features helpful gardening tips, how-to videos, and even recipes for cooking with the vegetables and herbs you grow in your garden.

While customer service is crucial, the core of the *Gardening without Guesswork* experience is the plants that Armstrong sells. Specific varietals are selected based on the local climate, so customers can have extra confidence that the plants they buy at Armstrong will grow well in their garden. Armstrong has its own nurseries where it grows the plants it sells to ensure quality.

The company also operates test gardens where new plant varieties are evaluated before they're sold in stores. According to James Russell, General Manager of Armstrong's growing facilities, this testing helps assure customers their plants will thrive. "Plant breeders are constantly coming up with new varieties. In order for them to be a part of what we do at Armstrong Growers, we have to prove them ourselves. So our test garden allows us to actually plant them in the ground and grow them through the season in an outdoor environment so we feel comfortable introducing those into our customers' yards."[4]

Russell emphasized that plants are selected for their durability. "Even if we find a variety that is stunningly beautiful, we have to make sure that it will perform for our customers." Some plants are tested for several years before the company begins selling them. "When a customer buys a plant from Armstrong," said Russell, "they can fully believe that this plant has been tested and will do well in their yard."

The Armstrong experience is designed around several guarantees. There's a traditional product guarantee in the form of a lifetime guarantee on all trees and shrubs. Plus, associates frequently offer implicit guarantees, such as assuring a customer that a specific care and feeding regimen will get your plants to grow in abundance.

The most important guarantee of all is Armstrong's *Gardening without Guesswork* philosophy. This doesn't take the form of a typical product guarantee, but, as you'll see, it's the foundation of Armstrong's Guaranteed Customer Experience.

The Definition of a Guarantee

A guarantee is a promise intended to provide assurance.

Jenny Dempsey received a couple of guarantees from associates at Armstrong Garden Centers. When she called, Kim gave her the assurance that it was okay to bring her calathea back to the store to get some advice. Sure enough, when Dempsey arrived, Carrie was available to assist her and already knew she'd be bringing the plant in.

Carrie provided assurance that Dempsey could revive her wilting plant. She spent time making suggestions and recommended a particular type of plant food. Sure enough, Dempsey's plant recovered.

Both Kim's and Carrie's assurances fit in with Armstrong's overall experience guarantee. The company's *Gardening without Guesswork* guarantee assures customers that they can get their garden or plants looking beautiful. It addresses a common customer problem—struggling to get plants to grow well—and promises a clear solution. The entire customer experience is pointed towards fulfilling that promise and helping customers get their plants to thrive.

There are other types of guarantees besides the ones Dempsey encountered. The Merriam-Webster dictionary defines a guarantee as both a noun and a verb.[5]

The noun is "an assurance of the quality of or of the length of use to be expected from a product offered for sale often with a promise of reimbursement." This is typically a product warranty, such as a new television that comes with a one-year warranty on parts and labor. The manufacturer offers the guarantee to assure customers the television will work as intended for at least one year, or the television will be repaired or replaced.

The verb is defined as "to assert confidently." You will often find this type of guarantee in a company's advertising, such as a commercial for a furniture store that loudly boasts, "We have the best selection of dining tables in town!"

Both types of guarantees have limitations when it comes to attracting and retaining customers.

Product warranties tend to focus on the product being free of defects. This is typically required by law anyway, regardless of whether the manufacturer or seller offers a written warranty. In the United States, every state except Louisiana has adopted Article 2 of the Uniform Commercial Code, which stipulates that products come with an implied warranty of merchantability. Specifically, products for sale must be of average quality and perform their intended function as advertised. So a new television is required to work properly, regardless of whether it comes with a written warranty.

Warranties against defects are so commonplace that they have little impact on the sales process. Customers are usually more concerned with other features and benefits the product offers, such as a new television's picture quality or compatibility with popular streaming apps.

Armstrong Garden Centers offers a lifetime guarantee on trees and shrubs, but that had no impact on Dempsey's decision to become a loyal customer. She wasn't aware of the lifetime guarantee when she went there to get help for her plant, and only learned about it when I mentioned it to her during our interview. In fact, returns under this warranty account for less than one percent of Armstrong's sales.[6]

Confident assertions, the verb form of a guarantee, can ring hollow with customers as well. There are advertisements everywhere promising low prices, great customer service, or 100 percent satisfaction. These don't carry meaning unless the companies making those promises back them up with something specific that has value to the customer.

Individual employees frequently make confident assertions. We've all heard employees tell us, "Don't worry, I'll take care of it," "Yes, that product will fix your problem," or "Our repair technician will be there between 9:00 am and 1:00 pm," only to have none of those things actually happen.

An experience guarantee goes beyond merely promising that a product won't break or that you have the lowest prices in town. It promises to solve a customer's problem, and then consistently delivers an experience that's as good or better than promised.

Experience guarantees can either be explicit or implicit, and both play a role in defining a great customer experience.

An explicit guarantee makes a clear promise and describes the remedy if that promise is not kept. Later in this book, you'll see examples of explicit experience guarantees, such as Osprey's All Mighty Guarantee and Briggs & Riley's Simple As That® guarantee. Both include a specific process to make things right for the customer if the promise is ever broken.

An implicit guarantee makes a clear promise without spelling out the remedy if the promise isn't kept. Buc-ee's, which you met in Chapter 1, creates an implicit guarantee that its restrooms will be clean by advertising clean restrooms. Should a Buc-ee's restroom ever fall short of that promise, there's an employee on hand to quickly clean it. Likewise, Armstrong's Gardening without Guesswork philosophy is an implicit guarantee that you'll become a confident gardener. As Dempsey can attest, helpful employees are available to get you back on track if your confidence wavers.

Whatever form it takes, an experience guarantee is a clear promise intended to assure customers that they'll have a great experience. It then provides a blueprint for an individual employee, a specific product, or even an entire company to consistently fulfill that promise.

The Benefits of Offering an Experience Guarantee

An experience guarantee helps you attract new customers, retain existing customers, and create evangelists who promote your business via word-of-mouth advertising.

Attract Customers

Do your sales and marketing teams struggle to describe what your company does, or what makes your product special compared to the competition?

One marketer I spoke with used every buzzword and bit of corporate jargon imaginable to explain her company's product. She went on for several minutes, but none of it made much sense until she finally said, "We help contact center managers automate routine tasks without having to learn to code."

Attracting new customers is difficult when you can't clearly explain what you do for them, how you'll do it, or why you're better than the competition.

Finding this clarity is a common challenge for companies. Marketers struggle to create advertising or website copy that speaks clearly to the problems customers are trying to solve. Salespeople default to pushing discounts instead of selling solutions. Business development executives pursue endless new revenue streams without first considering whether each opportunity is a good fit with the company's capabilities or existing product or service portfolio.

An experience guarantee provides clarity that shines like a beacon to potential customers. Travelers on a road trip see a Buc-ee's billboard advertising clean restrooms and instantly know what makes Buc-ee's stand out over other gas station convenience stores. People looking for a place to meet a friend for coffee are attracted to the spacious and comfortable seating area at The Simple Coffee House.

Desiree Heimann, vice president of marketing for Armstrong Garden Centers, understands its customers are worried about making their gardens look beautiful. "Our research has shown they have fear during every step of the process, from not knowing where to start, to asking dumb questions, to how to get the plants home without getting their car dirty or killing them."[7]

The company's *Gardening without Guesswork* guarantee speaks directly to that fear and assures customers they'll have a good experience. Recall that Jenny Dempsey wasn't sure where to start when it came to keeping her plants healthy, and she worried about asking dumb questions. Those fears quickly went away when she went to Armstrong to get help.

Retain Customers

How much could your company grow if it retained more customers? What would be the bottom-line impact for every customer saved?

An executive told me his company's growth had plateaued as it lost too many important clients, but he wasn't sure why they were leaving. He couldn't articulate what problem his company solved. Without a clear understanding of his clients' core problem, or a clear promise to solve it, the executive wasn't sure where his company fell short or what it could do better.

Customer retention is a common problem for many companies. For every customer you lose, you need to add one customer to replace that revenue and a second customer to increase revenue. That number expands quickly. If you have 100 customers and lose 20 of those customers per year, you'll need to add 21 customers that same year just to achieve a one percent growth rate.

Costs increase when retention rates are low. The marketing and sales teams need funding to keep looking for new customers, while the customer service team is kept busy trying to persuade unhappy customers not to take their business elsewhere.

Customers leave businesses for two main reasons. The first is that a competitor promised to do something that's important to the customer, and do it better than the customer's old company can, whether it's offer a lower price, greater convenience, or a unique service. The second reason customers leave is that they're upset about a service failure and no longer trust their old company to effectively solve their problem. This is a broken promise in the customer's mind, such as a product that doesn't work, a late delivery, or a rude customer service representative.

An experience guarantee can help you overcome these challenges and retain more customers. The guarantee promises you'll solve a problem customers really care about, which makes it more difficult for competitors to lure them away with a slightly better price, marginally better convenience, or an empty boast about great service. Fulfilling your promise will help you avoid service failures that prompt customers to search for alternatives.

My garden problem is tomatoes. I've struggled to grow them in the past and had only managed to harvest a handful each year. So, like Dempsey, I went to my local Armstrong Garden Center to get advice.

An associate named Andrew assisted me. He made several confident assertions about the right type of soil, fertilizer, and watering schedule I would need. Andrew helped me select the correct size tomato cages to help support the weight of each plant as it grew. He even gave me advice on picking out the right tomato plants and recommended against a few options that might not grow well in my garden. These assertions formed an implicit experience guarantee that I'd be able to grow an abundance of tomatoes.

The real test was what happened when I followed Andrew's advice. Had my tomatoes stagnated like they had in the past, I would have felt that Andrew didn't keep his promise. This disappointment would in turn make me less loyal to Armstrong and more likely to try out a different garden center the next time I wanted to work on my garden.

Fortunately, Andrew's advice was spot-on. I watched as my tomato plants grew larger than I'd ever grown tomato plants before. The plants bore an unbelievable abundance of juicy tomatoes that were absolutely delicious. Each tomato I picked that season reminded me of my Armstrong experience and reinforced my intention to shop there again.

Create Evangelists

Do customers actively tell family, friends, and everyone else they know about your company? Are the majority of online reviews about your company, products, or services glowingly positive?

One small business owner confided that she worried about her company's reputation. Every complaint or negative online review felt personal, so she tried to ensure that customers had nothing to complain about. She listened to feedback and worked hard to create a consistently great customer experience.

That customer focus helped her company earn a stellar reputation on Yelp, Google, and other online review platforms. People recommended the business to friends and family. The owner had to spend far less on advertising than her competitors, which increased her profit margins as the company continued to grow. She eventually acquired her biggest rival—a company that was going out of business because it had lost so many customers due to a poor experience.

Customer evangelists who do your sales and marketing for you can have a tremendous impact on customer growth. At the beginning of this chapter, I mentioned that Jenny Dempsey wrote about her experience with Armstrong Garden Centers on *Customer Service Life*, a popular blog in the customer service community. Dempsey herself has been recognized numerous times as a leading customer service professional, and she frequently speaks at conferences and on webinars. In other words, Dempsey is a customer service influencer who has become an evangelist for Armstrong Garden Centers.

She became a huge Armstrong fan because of the *Gardening without Guesswork* experience. Her plant is thriving, and she has much more confidence in her abilities, thanks to helpful advice from associates Kim and Carrie.

It's not only Dempsey who feels this way. The Armstrong Garden Centers location that Jenny visited has a four-star rating on Yelp, one whole star higher than the big box store nearby.

The Elements of a Great Experience Guarantee

Christopher Hart wrote in his book, *Extraordinary Guarantees*, that a great guarantee "is intended to force a company to deliver excellence, and fight to win and retain customer loyalty."[8]

While Hart's 1998 book focused on product or service guarantees, his description of an exceptional guarantee holds true for customer experience. Companies, departments, and even individuals that offer experience guarantees challenge themselves to deliver excellence that wins customers and keeps them coming back.

The Guaranteed Customer Experience model will help you construct an effective experience guarantee. You'll be able to attract customers, retain their business, and create evangelists from your biggest fans.

As we learned in Chapter 1, the starting point for a great experience guarantee is to identify a problem your customer is trying to solve. Examples include:

★ Buc-ee's: "I need to use the restroom."

★ The Simple Coffee House: "I need to meet a friend for coffee."

★ Armstrong Garden Centers: "I need to make my garden look beautiful."

An experience guarantee has three elements:

1. Promise
2. Action
3. Recovery

We'll cover each one in detail throughout this book, but here's an overview to start with.

Promise

The first element of an experience guarantee is a promise to solve the customer's problem. It gives customers assurance that a company, product, service, or individual employee will come through for them.

We'll cover promises in detail in Part II, including how promises attract customers and the elements of a great promise.

Action

The next element is taking action to fulfill your promise. Customers evaluate their experience based on whether or not you keep your word and actually solve their problems. A promise kept can strengthen customer loyalty, while a promise broken can create a lasting negative memory.

In Part III, we'll take a closer look at ways you can keep your promises, including the impact of a broken promise, steps you can take to keep more promises, and how to monitor the customer experience to ensure promises are kept more consistently.

Recovery

The final element of an experience guarantee is recovery. There will be times when a promise is not kept, or customers perceive that a promise was broken. This is when companies are most vulnerable to losing customers, and a solid recovery plan can help rebuild trust that your promises will be kept in the future.

Part IV focuses on why you need a service recovery plan and how to create an effective recovery plan.

Exercise: Evaluate Your Existing Guarantees

This chapter's exercise will strengthen your understanding of the broad definition of a guarantee. Your organization likely has existing guarantees, and taking a few moments to identify and evaluate some of them will start moving the Guaranteed Customer Experience from theoretical to practical.

Some existing guarantees might be clearly identifiable, such as a warranty or a slogan that includes the word "guarantee" in it. Others might be implicit guarantees that aren't as obvious, but fit the definition of an experience guarantee nonetheless.

Start by brainstorming a list of existing guarantees. These guarantees might exist at multiple levels of the organization or in multiple departments. For example:

★ Customer experience vision statements

★ Marketing slogans

★ Warranties against product defects

★ Satisfaction guarantees

★ Customer service standards

The next step is to evaluate each guarantee using the following questions:

1. What problem does this solve for the customer?

2. What promise does it make?

3. How often is that promise kept?

4. What is done to make things right if the promise is not fulfilled?

The strongest experience guarantees address a problem that customers care about and make a clear promise to solve it. Of course, that's only the beginning, because you must consistently keep that promise.

The exercise at the end of Chapter 1 asked you to identify a customer problem that you could solve. Now is a great time to go back to that exercise and determine whether there's already a guarantee in your organization promising to solve that problem.

The results of this exercise help you identify existing guarantees that are highly effective as well as those that need improvement. If there's an existing guarantee that addresses the customer problem you identified in Chapter 1, you can use this book to make that guarantee even stronger. If your organization doesn't have a guarantee addressing the customer problem, you can use that problem as a starting point to build a Guaranteed Customer Experience.

Once you complete this exercise, you're ready to move on to Part II, where we'll explore how to create a compelling promise that attracts more customers.

Chapter 2 Notes

1 Jenny Dempsey, "What Armstrong Garden Centers did right with feedback," Customer Service Life blog, January 3, 2020.

2 Armstrong Garden Centers website, accessed May 14, 2020, https://www.armstronggarden.com/about-us-home/careers-home/inside-our-culture.

3 Yelp reviews for Armstrong Garden Centers in Encinitas, California, accessed May 14, 2020, https://www.yelp.com.

4 James Russell, "Armstrong Test Gardens – Armstrong Garden Centers," armstronggarden YouTube video, March 14, 2012.

5 *Merriam-Webster Dictionary*, accessed online, https://www.merriam-webster.com.

6 Heather Larson, "Guaranteed success," *Garden Center* magazine, December 13, 2016.

7 Heather Larson, "Guaranteed success," *Garden Center* magazine, December 13, 2016.

8 Christopher W. Hart, Ph.D., *Extraordinary Guarantees: Achieving Breakthrough Gains in Quality and Customer Satisfaction*, Spire Group, Brookline, MA, 1998.

PART II: PROMISES

What will you do to solve your customer's problem?

Chapter 3
THE POWER OF A PROMISE

How do you get a new bed delivered to a remote location on short notice?

That's the problem my wife, Sally, and I faced. We own a vacation rental cabin called The Overlook, located in the Southern California mountain village of Idyllwild. A routine inspection had revealed one of the beds was broken.

Vacation rental guests tend to cause extra wear and tear on household furniture, so it was difficult to tell if the damage came from a single careless renter, or the cumulative impact of guests using the bed over several years. What we did know was the bed could not be repaired, so it needed to be replaced before our next guests arrived.

That was on a Sunday evening. We had just arrived at the cabin for a three-night stay, during which we planned to convert one of the bedrooms into a game room. This entailed receiving deliveries of new furniture, hauling away the old bedroom set to a donation center, and setting up the new room. There were also routine maintenance tasks and a few minor repairs to complete. Everything had to be finished by Wednesday morning so the cabin could be cleaned and readied for our next guests to arrive.

The broken bed created an unanticipated problem. The Overlook is a one-hour drive from the nearest town with furniture stores. We discovered the problem on Sunday evening, so stores were already closed for the day. We would have to go shopping on Monday, hope we could find something we liked, and then hope the bed could be delivered and set up by Wednesday morning at the very latest.

We worried. We worried about getting a replacement bed in time, how much it would cost, whether it would fit our decor, and how long it would last. We also worried about whether we'd have enough time get all the other projects completed before we had to leave.

You might recall from Chapter 1 that Amazon is excellent at solving the problem of needing to buy something quickly and conveniently. Even in a remote location like Idyllwild, we knew we could get light bulbs, a new coffee machine, or a throw blanket delivered in a day or two. But an entire bed? That seemed out of reach.

We decided to check anyway. A quick search brought up one highly-rated brand: Zinus. It had lots of attractive, stylish beds. Many had hundreds of ratings, with high marks for packaging, easy assembly, sturdiness, and overall value.

I checked the Zinus website to learn more about the company. It clearly specialized in helping people like us solve the problem of getting inexpensive, well-made furniture delivered quickly. The home page stated simply, "Mattresses, Bed Frames & Couches Delivered to Your Doorstep."[1]

There was a Zinus bed on Amazon that fit the bedroom's decor and was in stock. The price seemed impossibly low for a bed sturdy enough to survive more than a few weeks in a vacation rental, but all those reviews assured us the bed was well-designed and would last a long time. The Amazon website guaranteed delivery by Tuesday evening if we ordered right away.

A few clicks later and it was ordered. Now the waiting began.

Zinus and Amazon made a promise to solve our problem. Advertising from both companies led us to expect delivery of a stylish, sturdy, and easy-to-assemble bed on Tuesday evening. This provided some temporary relief, but we were still worried. Would all those promises be kept?

If Amazon and Zinus kept their promises, everything would be great. On the other hand, we'd be out of time to pursue alternatives if Tuesday came and went and we still didn't have a bed.

Sally and I felt a wave of relief when the delivery driver arrived at The Overlook around 8:00 pm Tuesday, with the bed packed in a long, flat box. Exhausted from a full day of doing our other chores, we decided to put the bed together the following morning. Both of us hoped it wouldn't take too long, since we needed to leave the cabin by 11:00 am.

The next day, we were surprised by a number of things.

The first was how easy the bed was to assemble. The parts were clearly marked with small, numbered stickers that made it easy to identify each piece and the sequence in which they went together. The package included a special ratchet tool—instead of the usual L-shaped wrench—that allowed us to fasten the bolts in seconds. Perhaps the biggest surprise of all was that the bed was incredibly sturdy and well-constructed.

What started as a minor panic—needing a bed in a hurry—turned into a major relief. The problem of needing a bed was solved. In fact, the bed looked great. It was a clear upgrade from the bed it replaced!

Zinus won itself two new fans.

How Promises Help Customers and Employees

A promise brings relief to worried customers and provides clarity to employees tasked with keeping it. This helps you win new customers and retain existing ones.

How Promises Help Customers

People have a lot to worry about. There are concerns about health, relationships, money, and work. They fret about politics, the economy, the environment, and the future in general.

Broader worries are compounded by more specific worries that cause customers to seek out specific products and services. Travelers on a road trip worried about getting to their destination safely also worry about finding a clean restroom. Gardeners worried about making their homes look beautiful also worry about keeping their plants alive. Sally and I were worried about creating a great experience for our guests, and then we had the added worry about getting a new bed in time.

Worrying is a psychological process for solving problems. Some degree of worrying can helpfully spur us into action to find solutions. However, the stress and anxiety associated with worrying increases when we continue to think about our problems, but are unable to identify a way to solve them.[2]

These worries impact our health. A survey of over 5,000 Americans conducted by Zinus revealed that worrying makes it difficult for 55 percent of people to fall asleep each night.[3] According to the Anxiety and Depression Association of America, more than 3 percent of the U.S. population suffers from Generalized Anxiety Disorder (GAD), which is characterized by persistent and excessive worrying. GAD symptoms include exhaustion, difficulty sleeping, increased heart rate, and gastrointestinal problems.[4]

A company, product, or even an individual employee who promises a solution can bring relief to a worried customer. Just as Sally and I felt better when we ordered the Zinus bed, customers feel hopeful that their problem will be solved. This feeling of relief is intensified when the promise is kept, such as when our bed was delivered and we were able to assemble it before our guests arrived.

Relief is a powerful way to create customer loyalty.

Research conducted by the Temkin Group revealed that relief is the top emotion experienced by customers after contacting a company with problems such as filing an insurance claim, investigating a billing error, or getting technical support. Customers who felt relief after an interaction were 34 percent more likely to want to do more business with a company, compared to those who still felt worried.[5]

Think about how you first found the companies where you're a loyal customer. You might have found your dentist after worrying about where to get your teeth cleaned with minimal discomfort. There's a good chance you first discovered that plumber you have on speed dial while worrying about a water leak. At work, your company might have been introduced to an important supplier because you worried about getting quality parts delivered on time.

The companies you met in previous chapters attract customers by promising relief from a variety of worries. Buc-ee's provides relief to customers worried about finding a clean restroom. Starbucks provides relief to customers worried about finding a convenient place to get a cup of coffee. Armstrong Garden Centers provides relief to customers worried about keeping their plants alive.

Zinus customers worry about finding the right balance of quality, price, and convenience. Freelance writer Zoe Sessums summed it up in a review of the popular Zinus Shawn bed frame on the *Architectural Digest* website. "I went to Amazon and looked for the bed frame that had lots of great reviews, wouldn't cost me three months of rent, and wouldn't take a doctorate to assemble."[6]

The Zinus website makes a number of assurances to address these worries. It promotes a customer experience where "every Zinus product sparks joy and delivers comfort direct to your doorstep."[7] Zinus also promises free shipping, a 100-night trial, and 24/7 support. Bed frames come with a five-year warranty against defects. The website proclaims having over 800,000 satisfied customers, which provides social proof that the company's assurances are valid.[8]

It's the promise of relief that prompts new customers to buy. Yet companies must deliver on that promise if they want to retain customers and have them become evangelists who recommend the company to others.

Keeping promises and earning customer evangelists is where Zinus shines. The bed frame we purchased for The Overlook has a 4.4-star rating (out of 5) on Amazon from over 500 reviews. Other Zinus beds for sale on the site have thousands of reviews and similarly high ratings. You can find positive recommendations of Zinus products from independent reviewers on influential websites such as those for CNN, POPSUGAR, and *New York Magazine.*

Add Sally and me to the list of evangelists who heartily recommend Zinus products. As I write, the new bed has been in place for several months. It's held up well and still looks great.

How Promises Help Employees

A promise can break down corporate silos and create tremendous clarity for employees. It can help them see beyond the individual tasks they have to complete and understand the bigger picture. Employees in customer-focused companies know the promises their company makes to customers, and they know the role they play in upholding those promises.

At Zinus, fulfilling the promise of inexpensive, high-quality *mattresses, bed frames, and couches delivered to your doorstep* starts with product design. According to Jen Cha, vice president of product, all products are designed with shipping and assembly in mind. "Zinus believes putting furniture together should be fun, not painful."

Cha explained how the focus on ease of assembly led Zinus to develop the innovative system where each piece has a number indicating the order in which it is assembled. "It's easy and intuitive to know which pieces go together," said Cha. "You almost don't need the assembly instructions!"

I asked Cha about the ratchet that came with our bed. It was a smart upgrade from the standard L-shaped Allen or hex wrench that comes with most furniture requiring assembly, because you can tighten each bolt quickly without removing and repositioning the wrench every time you turn it. The ratchet easily saved us 30 minutes on the assembly process.

Cha told me the idea came from Zinus's founder, Youn Jae Lee. "Other brands provide L-shaped wrenches for assembly, but he used to personally assemble every piece of furniture to gauge how easy it was. He wanted to make assembly easier and more convenient, so the team developed this tool. Even now, he assesses how easy a piece of furniture is to assemble before he approves it."

Promises influence employees in other customer-focused companies, too. At Buc-ee's, employees know that clean restrooms are part of the company's brand reputation, and they work hard to keep those promises. Armstrong Garden Center employees know they are a valuable part of the *Gardening without Guesswork* philosophy and go out of their way to give customers confidence in their gardening skills.

Employees who have little or no direct contact with customers often tell me they struggle to see their role in customer service. After all, it's someone in another department who hears about customer problems and solves them. But an experience guarantee makes it easier to get those employees focused on customers, too. As Jen Cha noted with the Zinus design process, product designers, manufacturers, and shipping teams all have a role to play in delivering an exceptional experience.

Even third-party partners, such as Amazon, contribute to the way customers feel about their interactions with the brand. Sally and I ordered the Zinus bed through Amazon for one very important reason: years of experience told us if Amazon promised the bed would be delivered by Tuesday, it would be delivered by Tuesday. In this way, Amazon helped Zinus fulfill its promise of a great bed frame at a great price delivered to our door.

I wouldn't have written about how wonderful Zinus is if the company hadn't kept its promises. The bed could have arrived late or damaged, it could have been difficult to assemble, it could have looked nothing like the bed I saw online, or it could have broken the first time a guest slept on it.

Zinus kept all its promises. The Overlook has two other bedrooms, and the beds and mattresses in each will eventually need to be replaced. Zinus will be the first place I shop when the time comes.

What Happens if You Don't Make a Clear Promise

Why should your customers buy from you? Does a clear and compelling answer quickly come to mind?

If you struggle to find the right words, just imagine how difficult it is for your customers to understand what makes your products or services special when there are so many other options available.

Zinus has a lot of competitors, but it stands out with a clear and convincing promise. The brand stands for style, quality, and convenience at exceptionally low prices, which is exactly what Sally and I were looking for. None of the company's competitors promised to solve our problem the way that Zinus did.

Zinus competes in the crowded mattress-in-a-box category, where companies sell mattresses online and ship them directly to customers in boxes that are almost too small to believe. A lot of these companies also sell bed frames and other related products. The websites for the most popular brands focused on price by promoting sales, special offers, and other discounts. None led with the convenience of direct shipping, the ease of selecting the right item, or the promise of a stylish bed, even though all of those companies could potentially provide those benefits.

Local furniture stores sell bed frames online and via their showrooms. (Local is a relative term, since the nearest stores are an hour's drive from our cabin.) A scan of their websites turned up a variety of approaches. Some focused on price, while others just displayed products without really promising anything. One store had a rotating banner on its website that promised the best price, the best service, and the best warranties in town—baseless claims that were hard to believe and undercut the store's credibility.

Other manufacturers sell bed frames on Amazon. This leveled the playing field for delivery, since Amazon promised the same two-day delivery for many beds it had in stock. The difference here was quality and ease of assembly. Reviews of Zinus beds consistently mentioned unbelievable quality for the price and described how quick and easy they were to assemble.

Articulating why customers should buy from you is a struggle for many companies. A marketer friend told me candidly that this is the biggest challenge he faces. His company has multiple product lines serving multiple markets with multiple competitors. It's hard to figure out what makes each product special or why customers should buy them. Each product operates under its own leadership, which makes it difficult to tie all the product lines together in a single, cohesive message.

Why do marketers struggle with something that seems so basic? I asked brand leadership expert Denise Lee Yohn for an explanation. Yohn is a sought-after keynote speaker and the author of the books, *What Great Brands Do* and *Fusion: How Integrating Brand and Culture Powers the World's Greatest Companies.*

Yohn explained that marketers face several pitfalls when crafting a clear promise that will attract customers. One is focusing on the product, not the customer. "Product-focused marketers have a lack of understanding of who their core customers are, and what problem they are trying to solve." These marketers might understand a product's features inside and out, but they're not quite sure how customers actually use them.

Another challenge is the pressure to increase revenue. "Companies can dilute the clarity of a promise in pursuit of growth," said Yohn.

A Zinus competitor initially attracted customers with a promise to make buying a mattress easy. The company offered just one mattress that it promised would lead to a better night's sleep, so customers wouldn't have to navigate through a showroom full of confusing choices. The mattress could be ordered online, shipped conveniently to the customer's door, and the customer would have 100 nights to return the mattress if they weren't fully satisfied. Today, that promise of simplicity has been virtually eliminated: the company now has three mattress models and multiple variations to choose from, introducing the same array of confusing choices the company initially derided.

A third challenge is product quality. A company might make a clear promise but, ultimately, let customers down. "The problem is products, services, or offerings don't fulfill the promise," said Yohn. Marketers realize this and feel pressure to invent new ways to convince customers to buy, which detracts from the clarity of the initial promise.

Convincing a customer to keep buying from you is a struggle if you don't consistently solve a customer's problem. A competitor can easily lure customers away with a slightly better price if your product or service is seen as a commodity. Other customers might try another brand just for the novelty if there's nothing particularly special about what you're offering. You'll be sure to lose customers when competitors promise to solve critical problems that you haven't addressed.

Sally and I have had other items delivered to The Overlook. One company, from which we purchased several pieces of furniture, has a lengthy promise statement on its website. The statement contains buzzwords such as technology, innovation, selection, and customer delight. Yet what the company is actually promising is fundamentally unclear.

The company lures customers in with a large selection of household items offered at low prices. Unfortunately, most of the items we purchased for The Overlook have been of poor quality and didn't last very long. You negate an item's low price when it wears out quickly and you have to replace it much sooner than a similar item that's only slightly more expensive.

Delivery was another hassle with this company. It took multiple phone calls and emails to coordinate a specific delivery date for a shuffleboard table we ordered for the cabin's game room. Then the table arrived damaged, which kicked off another logistical nightmare.

A supervisor promised to schedule a replacement table to be delivered on a date when we were at the cabin. The new table would be assembled for us, and the damaged table would be hauled away. But that promise evidently wasn't communicated to the logistics team, which delivered the replacement table with no prior warning on a day when no one was there. Rather than assembling the new table and removing the damaged one as promised, the new table was left in a large box outside the cabin. It took multiple phone calls, several days, and a manager's intervention to get the box picked up.

Low prices only count for so much. We will not order from that company again, and we have discouraged others from ordering as well.

Exercise: What Will You Promise That Will Set You Apart?

This exercise will help you identify a promise you can make to your customers. You might want to download the Guaranteed Customer Experience workbook to help with this exercise, if you haven't already. You can find it at guaranteedexperience.com/workbook.

Let's start by reviewing how a promise fits into the Guaranteed Customer Experience model:

1. Problem: Start by identifying a customer problem you can solve.

2. **Promise: Make a clear promise to solve your customer's problem.**

3. Action: Take action to solve the problem for your customer.

4. Recovery: Have a plan to make things right if you fail to keep your promise.

The exercise at the end of Chapter 1 was to identify a customer problem that you solve. This problem should be written as an "I need to" statement from the customer's perspective. For instance, the problem Sally and I faced at The Overlook was "I need to re-place this broken bed by Wednesday morning."

Now imagine a customer is sharing this problem with you in a conversation. They're worried about solving the problem and are looking for relief. What can you promise to help them feel better?

Write your promise on the worksheet. Don't worry about word-smithing the perfect statement. We'll cover that in Chapter 4. For now, just imagine you're speaking to the customer.

For example, let's put the promise Zinus made to Sally and me in a conversational format. "We can deliver a great-looking bed by Tuesday night. It fits your budget, it's designed to last for a long time, and you can assemble it quickly."

Notice the statement focuses on the problem first—getting the bed delivered on time. None of the other benefits would matter much if the bed took two weeks to arrive and our guests had to sleep on the floor in the meantime!

Denise Lee Yohn cautions companies to focus on a promise that makes you different from your competitors. "Your differentiation needs to be your lead," said Yohn. "Make it clear why customers should buy from you versus someone else."

This could involve making a promise that other companies don't make, or making a promise that your competitors can't keep. For instance, Zinus offers a 100-night trial, where you have up to 100 nights to return any of its products, but so do many of its competitors. The 100-night trial is nice, but it doesn't convince customers to choose Zinus over other companies offering the same thing. That's why Zinus's primary promise is the unique combination of convenience, style, and value that its competitors can't match.

Sally and I learned this lesson when we crafted a promise for our guests at The Overlook. Our original promise statement was *"Welcome to your mountain community retreat."* We envisioned a place where people felt at home, enjoyed the mountains, connected with the local Idyllwild community, and looked at our cabin as the perfect retreat. Yet after speaking with guests and prospective guests, we gained a deeper insight into the problem our specific customers were trying to solve.

The Overlook is located a short, 10-minute drive from the town center of Idyllwild, where guests can find art, gift shops, and restaurants. While the town center was what we imagined with the "community" part of our promise, we learned that guests who wanted that community experience consistently chose other cabins within walking distance of the town center. Our cabin couldn't promise a connection to the local community nearly as well as our competitors could.

The guests who chose The Overlook were focused on something else. They consistently said, "I need to rent a place in the mountains for a quiet weekend with friends or family." These guests didn't care as much about exploring the town; they were more interested in a home base for hiking, mountain biking, and other outdoor adventures during the day, and a place where they could relax and unwind at night.

This is where The Overlook stands out from other cabins on the market. There's a large deck with views that stretch for miles, and it's the perfect place to watch a gorgeous sunset. The kitchen is stocked with extra dishes, cooking tools, and large serving platters, so families can prepare meals together. Guests can entertain themselves with a ping pong table, shuffleboard table, puzzles, board games, and two TV rooms. There's even a secluded hot tub to help soothe away the aches and pains after a day of outdoor adventures.

Understanding the real problem our cabin solved helped us modify our promise just a bit. We took out the word, "community," and simplified it to *"Welcome to your mountain retreat."*

The vacation rental market in Idyllwild is extremely competitive, but The Overlook has been booked nearly every weekend since we made this Customer Experience promise.

Chapter 3 Notes

1   Zinus has changed its brand promise since I ordered the bed. As of November 24, 2020, the company's brand promise statement appears to be "Afford to be you," which promises customers affordable and stylish mattresses, bed frames, sofas, and other furniture.

2   Graham C. L. Davby, James Hampton, Jola Farrell, and Sue Davidson, "Some Characteristics of Worrying: Evidence for Worrying and Anxiety as Separate Constructs," Pergamon Press plc, 1991.

3   "Sleep Anxiety America Survey," Zinus, August 15, 2019.

4   "Generalized Anxiety Disorder (GAD)," Anxiety and Depression Association of America website, accessed June 9, 2020, https://adaa.org/understanding-anxiety/generalized-anxiety-disorder-gad.

5   Bruce Temkin, "Examining 10 Emotions, 8 Interactions, and Resulting Loyalty," *Experience Matters* blog, March 16, 2017.

6   Zoe Sessums, "What Makes This the Most Popular Bed Frame on Amazon?," *Architectural Digest*, September 11, 2019.

7   Zinus website, accessed November 24, 2020, https://www.zinus.com.

8   Zinus website, accessed June 9, 2020, https://www.zinus.com.

Chapter 4

THE ELEMENTS OF A GREAT PROMISE

Selling expensive equipment to businesses is a complex process.

There are a host of financial implications. Office copier machines, computer hardware, medical devices, and other high-end equipment all come with installation, operation, and maintenance costs that must be considered. Buyers need help to understand the expected return on investment and the impact of the purchase on cashflow.

Businesses usually rely on loans or other forms of credit to make large purchases. Much like a car dealership offers to finance customers, equipment dealers can increase sales by making financing options available to their customers, often by working with a financing partner.

GreatAmerica Financial Services is one such partner, providing financing solutions that help equipment dealers grow their businesses. The company works with each client to understand their unique needs, crafting solutions that help clients sell more equipment and increase revenue. Its core experience promise is simple: *"Sell more with financing solutions fit for your customers."*

With help from GreatAmerica, All Makes Office Equipment improved revenue by 20 percent and increased customer retention by 90 percent. All Makes sells and services office equipment such as printers and copiers and also provides office furniture and interior design services. GreatAmerica helped them combine monthly billing for office equipment, service, and supplies, so customers received one simplified invoice instead of multiple bills for different items. Much of the billing process was automated, saving valuable administrative time. The simplified billing allowed All Makes to increase sales by offering a total solution to customers' office needs for one affordable payment.[1]

Similarly, Advantage Technologies grew revenue by 15 percent per year after working with GreatAmerica. Advantage provides computer network design and management, cybersecurity, technical support, and other IT services to small businesses. GreatAmerica helped them implement a hardware-as-a-service model, where Advantage Technologies purchases computer hardware financed by GreatAmerica and rents it to customers. This simplifies hardware decisions for customers, who no longer have to purchase computer hardware on their own. It also allows Advantage Technologies to standardize the hardware its customers use, making service easier.[2]

Sound Incorporated increased sales by nearly five times in just one year after working with GreatAmerica. The voice and data, sound, security, carrier, and managed IT services company recognized that customers were shifting away from owning their hardware. GreatAmerica helped Sound Incorporated package all the hardware and services customers needed into one program, so customers could purchase a complete solution for one monthly payment.[3]

These success stories are just the tip of the iceberg for GreatAmerica. The customer-focused company succeeds by understanding its customers' problems and making a variety of promises to solve them.

This chapter looks at what makes a great experience promise. You'll discover the various types of experience promises and the elements that make a promise great. And you'll continue refining the promises you make to your own customers.

The Three Types of Experience Promises

Customer experience promises fall into three broad categories.

★ **Brand promises** tell customers what to expect from a company.

★ **Product promises** focus on what a particular product or service can do for customers.

★ **Personal promises** are commitments made by individual employees.

These categories are not prescriptive. You don't need a certain number of each type to create a terrific experience. While it's best to have just one brand promise (I'll explain why in a moment), companies often make multiple product promises to address a wide range of customer problems, and employees frequently make a variety of personal commitments when serving customers.

Brand Promises

A brand promise tells customers what they can expect from a company. It addresses the fundamental problem the company solves for its customers and is the foundation of the overall customer experience.

This promise is made at the organizational level. It covers multiple products and services under one over-arching commitment. Brand promises are often shared with customers through a company's sales and marketing initiatives and require coordination between multiple departments to ensure that the promise is fulfilled consistently.

The GreatAmerica brand promise is *"Sell more with financing solutions fit for your customers."* This clearly addresses a core problem faced by equipment dealers—the need to offer financing in order to sell expensive equipment—and promises to help dealers solve that challenge.

A brand promise and a company mission statement naturally have a close relationship in customer-focused companies. The mission statement reminds employees and other stakeholders why the company exists. The brand promise is an externally-focused expression of the mission that's written to speak directly to customers.

The GreatAmerica brand promise is based on its mission statement, *"We help our customers achieve greater success."* Joe Terfler, the company's chief financial officer, described how GreatAmerica employees use the mission statement to guide their daily work and deliver the brand promise. "Our employees care a lot about whether customers win," said Terfler. "We try to say 'yes' to our customers as much as we can." Teams work hard to understand each customer's unique needs and then craft a financing solution to help that customer improve sales.

The Armstrong Garden Centers promise of *Gardening without Guesswork* is another example of a brand promise. Like GreatAmerica, everything Armstrong does for its customers is based on its brand promise, whether that means training employees to provide knowledgeable service, selecting the right plants to sell in its stores, or offering classes to help gardeners become more confident.

Since the brand promise is intended to encapsulate the overall customer experience, companies should have just one. Multiple or unclear promises make it difficult to send customers a clear signal that you understand their problem and can solve it.

One company that struggled with multiple promises operated a park with zip lines, obstacle courses, and other challenging outdoor activities. The leadership team was divided on the brand promise. Was it "providing guests with memorable and exciting outdoor adventures," or was it "helping corporate clients and other groups build more cohesive teams through team-building events?" A focus on the outdoors would naturally lead the company to emphasize exhilarating outdoor experiences for visitors. On the other hand, a team-building focus would de-emphasize the outdoors and open up opportunities to create more indoor-based activities.

Choosing both created issues. What messages should the company share in its advertising? Who was the target customer? What types of experiences should the company offer? How many employees were needed, and what were those employees' responsibilities? Without a clear brand promise, leaders weren't able to answer those questions, and revenue stagnated.

This brings up another challenge many companies experience: what to do with all the mission, vision, values, marketing slogans, service standards, and other statements that companies generate? Doesn't a brand promise just add to the list of endless corporate-speak?

That's a real danger. All these statements create guidelines intended to influence employees' daily work. Employees get confused when they're asked to follow more than one guideline, especially when the various guidelines aren't aligned to point them in the same direction. Even worse, employees in many companies simply disregard all the statements, rendering the various missions, visions, values, and other slogans meaningless.

The solution is to simplify. In *The Service Culture Handbook*, I wrote about the importance of companies picking just one statement to guide employees in their daily work. That statement is called a *customer service vision* in the book. I've since renamed it a *customer experience vision* to encompass the entire customer experience.

A customer experience vision is a shared definition of an outstanding customer experience that gets everyone on the same page. If you choose to share it with customers, the statement can do double duty as the brand promise. For instance, Armstrong's *Gardening without Guesswork* is both a brand promise letting customers know what to expect, and a customer experience vision that guides employee actions.

You can learn more about customer experience vision statements and get step-by-step instructions for writing your own at toistersolutions.com/vision.

Product Promises

A product promise is tied to a specific product or service. This is more than just a warranty against defects; a strong product promise should create an experience guarantee for that product or service that's aligned with the company's overall brand promise.

GreatAmerica has many products and services tailored to the various industries it serves. For example, the product promise for its rental fleet financing program is *"Increase your sales and gain market exposure with rental fleet financing."* The company makes a slightly different product promise for the financing programs it offers to medical equipment manufacturers: *"Finance Programs and Solutions to make it easier for your dealers and distributors to sell equipment."* Both promises are an offshoot of the *"Sell more with financing solutions fit for your customers"* brand promise.

The company's SnappShot® mobile app is another example of a strong product promise. The app promises to help equipment salespeople improve sales by spending more time with customers and less time on administrative work.

Administrative work is a common challenge for salespeople. Inputting customer data into a customer relationship management (CRM) platform, generating detailed sales quotes, and helping customers fill out credit applications can all be time-consuming tasks. That's time that salespeople would rather spend on more productive activities, such as identifying prospects, making sales pitches, and closing deals.

GreatAmerica's SnappShot® app promises to save time by scanning a customer's business card to automatically input customer data. The app then allows salespeople to instantly generate sales quotes and calculate a customer's monthly payment, so the salesperson can share a price quote in the initial sales meeting. The app also allows salespeople to complete a customer's credit application on the spot, further reducing administrative time.

Other companies you've met in this book offer product promises as well. Buc-ee's promises travelers clean restrooms. Amazon promises to deliver orders by a certain date. Order a coffee on the Starbucks app, and you'll get a promise that the correct order will be ready by a certain time. All three companies are amazingly good at keeping those promises.

A product promise helps customers understand what makes that product special. It differentiates a specific product from similar options offered by competitors. When a company sells a line of products, a product promise helps customers identify the particular product that's right for their specific needs.

Several years ago, I switched business insurance providers. My previous company would take several days to answer a question about my policy, because very few employees understood that particular type of insurance product. The annual renewal was another hassle, since the company made me fill out a five-page document each year before my policy could be renewed.

The new company, Hiscox, promised to provide an insurance policy tailored to the needs of my specific business. I called and spoke to a helpful customer service representative who patiently answered all my questions. The premium was significantly less than my old policy, which the rep explained was because Hiscox better understood the risks involved with my type of business. Finally, the renewal process is a dream—Hiscox simply emails the updated policies at the end of the year and reminds me to let them know if anything about my business changed.

That product promise, a policy tailored to my business, caused me to break up with my old company and start doing business with Hiscox. I've been a loyal customer for several years now, since Hiscox has consistently kept its promise.

Personal Promises

A personal promise is a commitment made by an individual employee to solve a customer's problem.

Personal promises can be made by a wide variety of customer-facing employees. A salesperson selling manufacturing equipment might promise the equipment will give the factory higher output. A customer service representative might promise a customer's billing problem will be fixed. A delivery driver might promise the truck will be arriving at the customer's location by a specific time.

Employees who do not have frequent customer contact can also make personal promises. In some hotels, the housekeepers leave a card in each room with their name on it to take personal ownership of the room's cleanliness. If you purchase a new pair of jeans and find an "inspected by" sticker inside, that's a personal promise from someone that those jeans pass the company's quality standards. When you call a company and hear a recorded message informing you the call will be recorded for quality and training purposes, that's a promise that someone behind the scenes is supervising and training the frontline employee who answers your call.

GreatAmerica employees take their personal promises seriously. For example, all employees promise customers that they'll answer the phone within two rings. "We don't have voice mail," explained Jennie Fisher, senior vice president and general manager of GreatAmerica's office equipment group.

Employees work in a team environment and are cross-trained, so they can cover each other's responsibilities. "The person who answers the phone can help the customer 80 percent of the time," said Fisher. Each member of the team knows that a ringing phone takes priority over other tasks, since it's likely to be a customer in need at the other end of the line.

Keeping personal promises helps build trust. When you do what you say you're going to do, customers know they can count on you and, by extension, the product or service you're supporting and the brand you represent.

One unique challenge about personal promises is that the individual making the promise is often not the person who keeps the promise. For instance, let's say you go to an appliance store and purchase a new washing machine. The salesperson makes a variety of promises about the washer's performance, even though the salesperson didn't design or build it. The salesperson might also schedule delivery at a certain time and promise that the delivery crew will install the new machine and haul the old one away. The salesperson must trust that the product designers, manufacturers, and delivery teams will all do their jobs correctly.

Fulfilling personal promises like this requires teamwork. The salesperson will trust their colleagues if the product quality is consistently high and the delivery process works flawlessly. On the other hand, a poor-quality product or inconsistent deliveries reflect poorly on the salesperson. A customer will feel the salesperson broke their promise if the new washing machine doesn't work as intended, or if the delivery and installation process doesn't go smoothly.

What Makes a Great Experience Promise?

The quality of an experience promise is ultimately defined by how effectively it helps a business attract and retain customers. The promise must create a clear difference between you and the competition to be compelling enough for new customers to give you a try. And you must be able to fulfill that promise in order to retain customers and earn their future business.

There are three qualities in particular that make up a great experience promise. Experience promises must be:

★ Valuable (to the customer)

★ Specific

★ Realistic

Valuable Promises

An effective experience promise offers customers something they value, creating a clear point of difference between you and the competition.

GreatAmerica's promise to help equipment dealers increase revenue carries tremendous value. Companies typically finance the purchase of expensive equipment, so helping customers get easy access to financing overcomes a real hurdle to increasing equipment sales. Other finance companies might promise lower rates, but GreatAmerica offers more value by promising to craft financing solutions tailored to each individual customer's specific situation.

Customer-focused companies often promote value over price, even when they offer lower prices than the competition. Buc-ee's typically has lower gas prices than nearby competitors, but it attracts travelers by addressing a more urgent need with the promise of clean and spacious restrooms. Zinus wins customers by promising high quality and convenience, even when its higher-priced competitors promote sales and special deals. Hiscox provided a substantial savings on my insurance premium, but they won my business by promising to understand my company's unique needs.

Promising better value than your competitors allows you to hold the line on prices, even if your company does charge more. GreatAmerica earns the right to charge more than other financing companies, because it delivers better results. Armstrong Garden Centers typically has higher prices than big box stores, but customers are willing to pay a premium to get professional advice and buy plants proven to thrive in their local area. The Simple Coffee House charges a premium for its coffee, but it offsets higher prices by creating a spacious and comfortable place to meet friends or get work done.

Specific Promises

Experience promises are more effective when they promise something specific. This makes it easier for customers to understand what they're being promised and why it's valuable. A specific promise also makes it easier for employees to understand what they're expected to do.

Notice that GreatAmerica's brand promise doesn't promote a generic concept like "great results" or "improve your business." It specifically tells customers that they will increase sales when they use GreatAmerica's financing solutions.

Let's look back at some of the promises made by other customer-focused companies introduced in this book. Each one addresses a specific problem:

★ Buc-ee's promises clean restrooms.

★ The Simple Coffee House promises a great place to meet a friend.

★ Amazon promises to deliver the right product on time.

★ Armstrong Garden Centers promises to make you a more confident gardener.

★ Zinus promises to deliver a mattress, bed frame, or couch to your doorstep.

Promises that are not specific leave room for misunderstanding and create a higher possibility that the customer will be disappointed. This is a particular challenge when making personal promises.

For example, a customer service rep might tell a customer, "I'll get back to you right away." But the customer and the employee might have different interpretations of what the phrase "right away" actually means. The customer might expect "right away" to be within the hour, while the employee might believe it means the next day. If the hour comes and goes without the customer getting the requested information, the customer would feel that the employee broke their promise.

Another common example of a promise that lacks specificity occurs when a customer is given a range of dates and times:

★ "Your order will arrive within two to four days."

★ "We'll have the repair done in two or three hours."

★ "Your table will be ready in 15 to 30 minutes."

Customers tend to hear the first part of the range and ignore the rest. If you tell a customer their order will arrive within two to four days, many customers will look for it to arrive on day two and be disappointed if it doesn't. A better approach is to promise the customer their order will be delivered "within four days," so there's less room for misunderstanding.

Companies typically schedule service appointments in four-hour windows. This creates two problems. The first is similar to the issue just described, where a customer who is given an appointment window of 8:00 am to 12:00 pm tends to hear the earlier time and begins to get anxious if the technician isn't there by 8:15 am. The second problem is that customers often expect the service call to be *concluded* by the later time, so an appointment window of 8:00 am to 12:00 pm might make the customer think they're free to make plans after 12:00 pm. This creates a service failure if the technician doesn't arrive until 12:00 pm and the service call ends up taking two hours.

A better strategy for appointment setting is to make more precise promises. This includes explaining how long the service call is expected to take. Elite companies offer a specific appointment time rather than a range, so customers know exactly what to expect. For example, they tell a customer, "Our technician will arrive at 10:00 am, and the appointment can take up to two hours, so expect the service call to last until 12:00 pm." That level of detail gives customers much more confidence in the company and leaves less room for a service failure—as long as the company keeps its promise.

When a restaurant customer is told their table will be ready in 15 to 30 minutes, there's yet another wrinkle. As in the previous examples, customers will start to get anxious when they've been waiting for 15 minutes. Plus, restaurant customers can see other guests being seated ahead of them. They might perceive a sense of unfairness if a party arriving later gets seated before them. Once again, a more specific promise can alleviate some of those concerns. "We'll have your table ready within 30 minutes. There are six of you, so we're waiting for two tables to open up so we can comfortably seat you all together."

Realistic Promises

The ability to consistently keep promises is one of the most important factors setting a company apart from the competition. This requires promises to be realistic enough that you can keep them consistently.

Take something as simple as food delivery. We live in a golden age where we can go online or open an app on our phone and order a meal to be delivered to our home within the hour. Many restaurants and delivery services even let you schedule the delivery for a particular time. Customers are given an estimated delivery time when they place an order, which is a valuable and specific experience promise.

Mountain Mike's Pizza in my neighborhood aces the process. The pizza tastes amazing because they use high-quality, fresh ingredients, but what really sets Mountain Mike's apart from other delivery options is the uncanny accuracy of its delivery promise. I can open my phone at 2:00 pm and order a Mountain Mike's pizza to be delivered at 6:30 that evening. My experience as a longtime customer gives me confidence that a delivery driver will be placing a fresh, hot, delicious pizza on my doorstep at precisely 6:30 that evening.

Other restaurants don't stand a chance with their inconsistent delivery service. A 30-minute delivery promise is broken when 45 minutes have passed and the meal hasn't arrived. A delivery promise for 7:00 pm is broken when it's 7:15 and there's no sign of the driver.

Promises only carry meaning if you can keep them, and promises backfire if a company routinely fails to deliver. There's a growing list of restaurants where I won't order food for delivery, because I know I simply can't count on them in the same way that I absolutely know Mountain Mike's will come through.

This is where product warranties routinely fall short. They're intended to give customers peace of mind. Yet the process for getting warranty service is often cumbersome, overly complicated, and full of hidden costs.

For example, my wife and I obtained a home warranty when we bought our home. The real estate agent promised it would protect us in the event something major went wrong, such as an appliance failure. Sure enough, our heater went out just a few months after we bought the home, so we called the home warranty company.

The company couldn't send a technician out for a week. We learned that despite the warranty, we'd still have to pay a service fee for the visit (this was buried in the fine print of our warranty contract). Once the technician determined the problem, it could be another week or two for the necessary parts to get ordered and for the technician to return and make the repair.

Peace of mind was instantly out the window. We ended up calling a local repair technician on our own and got the heater working again later that day. Saving a few bucks on the repair wasn't going to make up for going without heat for up to three weeks!

In Part III, we'll cover exactly how to ensure your promises are realistic. For now, let's go back to some of the promises you identified in Chapter 3 and see how we can make them even more effective at attracting and retaining customers.

Exercise: How can you make your promises great?

This exercise will help you further refine the promise you identified at the end of Chapter 3. Start by deciding which category your promise fits into:

★ **Brand promise:** what customers can expect from your organization.

★ **Product promise:** what customers can expect from your product or service.

★ **Personal promise:** what customers can expect from you.

The next step is to evaluate your promise against the three elements of a great experience promise.

Is your promise:

★ Valuable to your customers?

★ Specific?

★ Realistic?

The best way to answer those questions is to get feedback from actual customers. Focus groups, surveys, and one-on-one conversations can all help you create a promise that's meaningful to your target audience.

For example, one of my clients told me she needed a way to reinforce the skills taught in my customer service training class. We brainstormed different ideas and came up with a weekly email reminder. Each week, I promised to send her employees an email with one tip that reminded them of something we covered in the class.

The weekly email met all three elements of a great product promise. It was valuable to my client, because it solved her problem of needing to reinforce concepts from my training class. It was specific: one tip, via email, once per week. Setting up the email was easy to do, which also made it realistic.

We tested it out, and it worked so well that I decided to make the weekly email available to anyone who wanted it. I quickly learned that other customer service leaders faced a similar challenge. Many told me they needed an inexpensive and convenient way to reinforce customer service skills with their team.

Today, the email is called Customer Service Tip of the Week. The promise is simply, "Sharpen your skills with weekly customer service reminders." You can sign up for free here: toistersolutions. com/tips.

The three questions can also help you re-evaluate some of your organization's existing guarantees. (Recall that we identified some of those guarantees at the end of Chapter 2.) Repeat the exercise above for each one, first identifying whether it's a brand, product, or personal promise.

Next, use the three questions to identify areas of strength, as well as opportunities for improvement.

★ Is the guarantee valuable to your customers?

★ Is it specific?

★ Is it realistic?

Your review might reveal that your guarantee needs to be reworded or even focused on a completely different promise.

I used to include an explicit, written guarantee in all my customer service consulting proposals. The guarantee told potential clients that I'd make it right or refund their fee if they weren't satisfied with my services.

After talking to a lot of clients about what they truly valued, I realized my guarantee wasn't helping me land any business. They weren't worried about whether I'd make things right—that was already implied in our agreement. What my clients were really worried about was making the complex problem of building a customer-focused culture more easy and manageable.

When I decided to put my entire culture-building process in a book called *The Service Culture Handbook*, I used my clients' feedback to write a new guarantee. It's an implicit guarantee right there in the subtitle: *"A Step-by-Step Guide to Getting Your Employees Obsessed with Customer Service."*

The book has sold well, because the new guarantee promises to solve a problem clients are actually worried about.

Now it's your turn. Try writing a new experience guarantee or revising one you already have. Once you've completed that exercise, you'll be ready to move on to Part III, where we'll discuss how to take action to keep your promises.

Chapter 4 Notes

1 "How a Bundled Strategy Helped All Makes Office Equipment Co. Increase Revenue and Margins by over 20%," GreatAmerica website, accessed July 17, 2020, https://www.greatamerica.com/office-success-stories/all-makes-office-equipment-co.

2 "Success Story: Advantage Technologies," GreatAmerica website, accessed November 25, 2020, https://www.greatamerica.com/technology-success-stories/advantage-technologies.

3 "Sound Incorporated Case Study," GreatAmerica website, accessed November 25, 2020, https://www3.greatamerica.com/sound-incorporated-case-study.

PART III: ACTION

How will you keep your promises?

Chapter 5
THE IMPACT OF BROKEN PROMISES

Business looked bleak for Domino's in early 2009.

The 2008 fiscal year had been tough for the chain of pizza restaurants. Revenue was down 2.6 percent from the prior year. The company relies heavily on franchise operators, yet it had a net decrease of 108 franchises in the United States. An audit revealed that 12 percent of the company's 1,200 franchise locations worldwide were chronically underperforming.[1]

The company's problems continued to grow as the year went on. In April 2009, a video of two franchise employees defiling customer orders went viral. Among other disgusting acts, one employee was filmed putting cheese in his nose before putting it on a sandwich. The video led to the employees' arrests and a lot of grossed-out customers.[2]

Customers were already widely dissatisfied with the quality of Domino's pizza. In a 2009 consumer survey conducted by research firm Brand Keys, the company tied Chuck E. Cheese for worst-tasting pizza among the major pizza chains in the United States.[3]

The company's problems can be traced to a string of broken promises. Think about what you expect when you order a pizza for delivery: the pizza will arrive on time, taste good, and look like the pizza you ordered.

Domino's initially built its reputation around fast delivery. Until 1993, the company had offered a "30 minutes or less guarantee" on deliveries. The original guarantee promised customers a free pizza if it wasn't delivered within 30 minutes of placing their order. The guarantee was later changed to give customers $3 off their total.

The guarantee had many critics, as delivery drivers were accused of driving recklessly in order to meet the 30-minute promise. Domino's finally eliminated it in 1993 after facing two high-profile lawsuits when one delivery driver killed a motorist in a crash, and a second delivery driver severely injured another in a separate incident.[4]

Fifteen years later, the company discovered an innovative way to set delivery expectations. In early 2008, Domino's rolled out the Pizza Tracker™, an online tool allowing customers to track their pizza from the time it was ordered until it was delivered to their door. The tool also included a way for customers to submit feedback about their order—feedback that went straight to the store manager.[5]

The Pizza Tracker™ might have helped Domino's do a better job of keeping its delivery promises, but the company still failed to keep its basic promise of serving high-quality pizza. Domino's CEO, Patrick Doyle, admitted some years later, "When we did consumer tests, if they knew the pizza was Domino's, they actually liked it less than if they just thought it was a random unbranded pizza."[6]

In late 2009, the company offered a mea culpa in a new advertising campaign. One video produced by the company shared blunt feedback from customer focus groups and surveys. "Where's the love?" asked one customer featured in the video. "There doesn't feel like there's much love in Domino's pizza." Another customer said, "Domino's pizza crust, to me, is like cardboard."

Doyle directly addressed the feedback in that same video. "You can either use negative comments to get you down, or you can use them to excite you and energize your process of making a better pizza. We did the latter."

That video, and other Domino's commercials released during the ad campaign, offered customers a new promise. The company had listened to customer feedback and extensively reworked its recipes. Domino's promised its pizza was actually good again!

The promise of better-tasting pizza was real, and customers took notice. Domino's attracted positive publicity for its better-tasting pizza, and customers were increasingly willing to give it another try. Same-store sales rose 14 percent in the first three months of 2010.[7]

There was one more broken promise that Domino's took aim at fixing. The pizzas shown in commercials and other advertising were not how a pizza really looked when it showed up at your doorstep.

A video released by Domino's in July 2010 showed a behind-the-scenes look at how pizza commercials were filmed. People dubbed "food stylists" used an array of tricks to make the pizza look better on camera. Pepperoni slices were hand-cut and painstakingly arranged to make the slices look evenly distributed. Torches crisped the edge of the crust and heated the cheese to make it stringier. Hidden screws secured the pizza to a board, so the rest of the pizza would stay in place when a hand model pulled out a slice.[8]

The company announced it would begin using photos of real pizzas in its advertising. It launched a "Show Us Your Pizza" campaign, inviting customers to submit their own photos of Domino's pizzas.

CEO Patrick Doyle addressed one poor-looking photo in a commercial. A customer submitted a picture of a Domino's pizza with its toppings stuck to the underside of the box lid, as if the pizza had been squished inside the box. "This is not acceptable," said Doyle. "You shouldn't have to get this from Domino's. We're better than this."

Doyle then reiterated the company's commitment to keeping promises. "I'm Patrick Doyle. I'm the CEO of this company. We're not gonna fail. We're not gonna deliver pizzas like this. I guarantee it."

All these changes aimed at keeping promises paid off. By the end of 2010, revenue had increased 12 percent after two straight years of declines. The company continued to grow. And in 2018, Domino's finally surpassed its longtime rival, Pizza Hut, in total sales in the United States.

How Broken Promises Cost You Customers

In 2010, while Domino's Pizza was starting its resurgence, Matt Dixon and his colleagues at the Corporate Executive Board published the results of a study on customer loyalty in *Harvard Business Review*. The study highlighted research conducted over the course of several years and reached a startling conclusion: delighting customers does not increase customer loyalty.[9]

"The conventional wisdom out there was that at times of need when a customer reaches out to you with a problem, it's not enough to do what they expect you to do," said Dixon. "What we found was that those customers who were surprised and delighted and wowed were no more loyal than customers whose expectations were simply met."

The study found that keeping promises was the best way for a company to retain its customers. "There's a lot of good that we as companies can do by simply delivering the basics," Dixon told me. "Delivering what the customer expects, and delivering it in a consistent and predictable way."

The results of the study were later shared in a 2013 book Dixon co-authored with Nick Toman and Rick DeLisi called *The Effortless Experience*. The book expanded on the 2010 *Harvard Business Review* article and revealed some new insights on how broken promises drive customers to take their business to the competition.

One unexpected finding showed that customers are far more likely to be disloyal than loyal after a customer service interaction. The biggest driver of disloyalty was requiring customers to make more than one contact to resolve an issue. Those customers were

2.5 times more likely to take their business elsewhere than customers who had a neutral experience.[10]

Think of a time when you had to contact a company's customer service department over and over again to resolve an issue. Perhaps it was a promised refund that never materialized. You might have taken time off from work to meet a repair technician at your home, only to discover the technician didn't have a required part and would have to come back the next day.

These incremental broken promises are maddening. The initial problem represents a broken promise in the form of a defective product or service. Each failed attempt to resolve the issue represents an additional broken promise, as customers reasonably expect companies to quickly and conveniently solve the problem. Every contact adds an additional layer of frustration, and it becomes increasingly difficult to trust the company's ability to make things right.

Broken promises do more than just cause customers to head to the competition. Customers who encounter broken promises tell others about their experience. They post negative online reviews and complain on social media. The top reason customers complain on Twitter is having to wait too long for a response to a customer service issue, or receiving no response at all.[11]

The Domino's turnaround story is impressive, but the company still has work to do. An analysis of over 17,000 Yelp reviews of Domino's locations from June 2019 to June 2020 shows an overall rating of just two stars. The majority of the negative reviews focus on broken promises such as late deliveries, longer-than-expected wait times for pick-up, and incorrect food orders.

The company has added new features to the experience in recent years. You can get a pizza delivered to any number of "Domino's hot spots." These are popular locations where people gather, such as parks and beaches, that don't have a physical address. The company offers "Carryout Insurance," where it will replace a pizza free of charge if it's damaged after a customer picks it up, even if the damage is the customer's fault. Yet the Yelp data makes it clear that keeping its most basic promises is the best thing the company can do to bolster its reputation.

Keeping promises should be simple, shouldn't it? Customers struggle to understand why a company that specializes in pizza delivery can't consistently deliver the specific pizza they ordered on time and make it taste good!

What executives frequently fail to understand is the impact broken promises have on customer loyalty. In many cases, broken promises are not tracked, despite the proliferation of customer surveys and other data. In other cases, the cost of those broken promises isn't clear, so fixing them isn't urgent.

Let's use another form of delivery as an example: hotel room service. As a frequent traveler, I'll sometimes order room service when I arrive at a hotel after a long day on the road. The person who takes my order invariably gives me an estimated time when the order will be delivered. That delivery estimate is a personal promise, and how this promise is kept influences the quality of my experience.

A typical estimated delivery time is 30 minutes. I order room service when I'm tired and hungry from a long day of travel, so I'm counting on the hotel to keep its promise and solve my problem of needing a convenient way to get dinner.

I'll be disappointed if the order takes longer than 30 minutes to arrive. Unfortunately, I've had many experiences where it gets to be 45 minutes and there's still no sign of my food, which prompts me to call guest services to check on the status of my meal.

This is where Dixon's research on the impact of repeat contacts comes into play, as that second call to guest services means there's virtually no chance of a positive experience by now. The food is late, and I'm having to work hard to get the issue resolved.

It's also a problem if the order arrives early. A promised delivery time of 30 minutes tells me I have time to jump in the shower and freshen up. It leads to awkward moments if the room attendant arrives in 20 minutes and I'm just drying off.

Keeping that simple promise, to deliver the meal in 30 minutes, is the key to a great guest experience. A late or early delivery makes me focus on the inconvenience. That's the part of the experience that will stand out as the strongest factor in my impression of the hotel. An on-time delivery keeps my focus where it should be: relief as I enjoy a delicious room-service meal in the comfort of my hotel room after a long and tiring day of travel.

Companies can also fail customers by breaking promises that aren't explicit. Most gas stations don't explicitly promise clean restrooms, yet customers are inevitably disappointed to find a restroom that appears to be straight out of a horror film. Stores selling plants and gardening supplies rarely promise to have helpful employees who are knowledgeable about gardening, yet customers reasonably expect to find employees who can help.

A failure to keep implicit promises can cost your company business. For example, I purchased a small clock that included a wireless charging pad for my phone. An implicit promise that comes with an electronic device like this is that it will include a power cord, so it can be plugged into a standard wall socket. I was disappointed to discover that the clock did not come with a power cord—after I had already unboxed it and tried to set it up.

Nowhere did the company make an explicit promise to include a power cord. It wasn't mentioned in the online product description or even on the box. Yet just as important was the absence of a warning that I would have to purchase a power cord separately.

I promptly returned the clock and searched for similar products made by other companies. The one I ultimately purchased also did not include a power cord (is this a trend?), but this company shared a clear warning in the product description that the power cord was sold separately. They even promoted a package deal including a power cord for a reduced price. By simply calling out this unusual circumstance, the company avoided creating an implicit promise about the product's features and prevented customers like me from being disappointed.

Falling short of expectations forms a lasting memory in the customer's mind. A customer might have nine perfectly acceptable experiences, but if the tenth is a failure, that's the one that stands out.

The Peak-End Rule explains how these negative memories are formed. The rule states that customers tend to remember two critical moments in their overall experience. One is the part of the experience that differs the most from normal (the peak). The other is the last experience they had (the end).

A broken promise creates a negative peak in the customer's experience, whether it's a defective product, a call that's not returned, or a late food delivery. As we'll discover in Part IV of this book, that peak will also be the last impression the customer has with a business unless the company does something to recover.[12]

Customer-focused companies work tirelessly to avoid broken promises. And when broken promises do occur, they move quickly to fix them.

What Happens if You Don't Fix Broken Promises

Occasional broken promises are inevitable. Try as you might, products will sometimes be defective, services will fall short, and employees will make mistakes. The real challenge businesses face is making sure those broken promises don't become a chronic issue.

I've profiled a number of companies in this book that are great at keeping promises to solve problems. There was another company, a popular men's clothing retailer, that I hoped to include among these examples. Unfortunately, the more I researched, the more broken promises I found.

The retailer operates under a brand promise that they will take the pain out of shopping for men's clothing by helping customers find the perfect size and fit. You start by completing an online profile to identify your size in various garments, such as slacks, blazers, and dress shirts. Many items come in various fits, from the snug "tailored" fit, to the slightly roomier "regular" fit, so your profile includes your preferred fit in each type of garment. The company also has retail stores you can visit to try on different size, fit, and style options with the help of a knowledgeable associate.

The promise is attractive, but the company has recently struggled to deliver. A friend of mine told me he stopped doing business with them after receiving multiple orders with items that were either too big or too small. Similarly, I ordered a new blazer in my usual size that turned out to be significantly smaller than other blazers I had tried on from the same company. This came on the heels of a pair of chinos I ordered that were significantly tighter than the pair I'd tried on in the store. My friend and I both found ourselves returning purchases, disappointed by the company's broken promises.

There are many ways consistently broken promises hurt companies. The largest and most obvious repercussion is losing customers. My search for enthusiastic customers to interview about this brand turned up many former customers who had been excited about the brand's core promise, but stopped ordering after being disappointed too many times.

Upset customers turn to Yelp and other online review sites to share negative feedback—feedback that might dissuade future customers from trying out a business. For instance, the clothing company's retail stores averaged 3.5 stars on Yelp reviews from June 2019 to June 2020, with 21 percent of the reviews mentioning poor customer service and 15 percent of the reviews describing poor-fitting or low-quality clothing.

Consistently broken promises also increase costs. Poor-fitting clothing leads to more customer returns, which increases the shipping and labor costs associated with return orders. Clothes that aren't properly sized must be liquidated, creating an additional expense for a company that's already losing money.

That clothing company isn't alone in its customer service woes. A well-known cable company announced a plan to spend $300 million and hire 5,500 customer service employees to fix its poor customer experience ratings. It even hired a marketing consultant to put together a series of showcase events for customer experience authors and speakers like me, in an attempt to convince us to stop sharing so many negative examples in our publications and presentations. (I declined the invitation, as the company had yet to show any real improvement in the eyes of its customers.) That colossal investment could have been avoided if the company had focused on keeping its promises to begin with.

Many once-venerable retail brands have filed for bankruptcy in recent years due to chronically broken promises. Sears, J.C. Penney, J. Crew, Neiman Marcus, Forever 21, Toys "R" Us, Pier 1, and many others once had legions of loyal customers. Poor inventory management, poor product quality, and poor customer service, combined with crushing debt, brought down all these once-great businesses.

There's a good chance a few companies have landed on your own "no buy" list. They've disappointed you so many times that you go out of your way to avoid doing business with them, even if it means paying more somewhere else.

Why don't these companies fix these chronic issues that drive away so many customers?

The impact of broken promises is often hidden in a company's financial data. Executives can see top-line revenue and overall expenses, but it takes a little more investigation to identify how a broken promise impacts those figures.

Running that calculation in a clear and credible way is an important part of implementing a Guaranteed Customer Experience. Attaching a specific dollar value to broken promises is often needed to convince executives to approach customer experience with a sense of urgency.

Exercise: Calculate Your Customer Math

Customer experience pioneer and bestselling author Jeanne Bliss suggests businesses calculate their "customer math" to understand the impact of customer experience on the bottom line.

"At the end of the day," says Bliss, "we are in business to grow our business." Many companies obsess about customer acquisition, but Bliss recommends companies also pay careful attention to customer retention.

"The key is to do a common version of the math," says Bliss. She suggests members of the executive team, including the chief executive officer (CEO) and chief financial officer (CFO), meet to agree upon a single net customer value metric and a consistent way to run the calculation. That metric, says Bliss, needs to be reviewed just as frequently as other important business drivers, whether it's at a weekly executive meeting or a monthly business review.

The metric has three components:

★ **Customer Base:** What is our customer value at the start of the period?

★ **Acquisition:** What is the value of new customers?

★ **Churn:** What is the value of customers we lost?

Calculate your change in net customer value by adding the value of new customers to the customer base you had at the start of the period (week, month, quarter, etc.) and subtracting the value of customers you lost during the same period. (You'll find a worksheet to help you in the workbook at guaranteedexperience.com/workbook.)

Start with the number of customers at the beginning of the period being tracked, and multiply that by your average customer value.

This is easy to do in some businesses, such as the software-as-a-subscription industry, where customers pay a set price per month to access your software. The value of your customer base would simply be the number of paying customers multiplied by the average price those customers paid.

The calculation can get a little complicated in other types of businesses. A consumer products company might have a line of ten products that are sold to various wholesale customers at a discount and sold direct to consumers at the full retail price. Other companies have multiple business units that each sell to completely different customers.

Nevertheless, Bliss recommends companies create a metric that represents the company's entire customer base. Looking at business units or product lines individually without seeing the big picture can hide customer experience issues that span the entire organization.

"The CEO needs to care, as an enterprise, are we earning and keeping more valued customers than we're losing," says Bliss. "That means we all have to have one common version of new, lost, or lapsed, and be consistent in how we roll it up and present it to the CEO. It doesn't mean that individual product categories can't present their numbers, but we've got to roll it up."

Once you've identified the value of your customer base at the start of the period in question, calculate the value of customers you added for that time period. This calculation is run the same way as your customer base, by multiplying the number of new customers added times the average value of those customers.

Finally, calculate the value of customers lost by multiplying the number of lost customers by their average value.

Now you'll have the three data points you need to create your net customer growth metric. The formula looks like this:

customer base + customers added - customers lost = net customer value

Observing the change in net customer value over time gives you a more accurate picture of the impact that promises, and broken promises, have on customer acquisition and retention.

Here's a simplified example. Let's imagine that a company had 10,000 customers at the start of the month. Those customers averaged $50 in monthly revenue, or $500,000 total. Spread out over a full year, that equals $6,000,000 in projected annual revenue.

During the month, the company adds 1,000 new customers. That seems pretty good, since that equals 10 percent growth in just one month. The chief marketing officer would probably be tempted to trumpet this success in their monthly report!

But wait: we need to calculate the value of the customers added. Those 1,000 new customers were incentivized with a special discount, so their average monthly value was just $25, or $25,000 total. Those new customers are substantially less valuable than the $50 average of the existing base. This might set off alarms among the executive team, since offering substantial discounts to entice new customers can be a sign that the company's value proposition is not enough to bring in customers at full price.

Here's where accounting for the value of lost customers paints an even more complete picture. During that same month, the company lost 500 customers. Unlike the new customers, the lost customers were largely paying full price, and most had added additional products and services. The average monthly value of the customers the company lost was $75, meaning those customers had been spending more than the $50 average. That puts the total value of lost revenue at $37,500 ($75 x 500 customers).

Now we have the data we need to calculate the change in net customer value for the month:

$500,000 (current base)
+ $25,000 (new customers)
- $37,500 (lost customers)
_____
$487,500 net customer value

Despite adding 1,000 new customers, the company's net customer value actually *decreased* by $12,500 for the month in this example.

That 2.5 percent decline is far more telling than just looking at customer acquisition alone.

This metric can make executives uncomfortable. For example, the chief marketing officer for the company in the previous example might feel threatened if the addition of 1,000 new customers was not celebrated and was instead called into question. Product development, operations, and customer service leaders might be tempted to blame each other for lost customers, rather than working together to identify and fix the root cause. Make sure you involve the entire executive team, including your CEO and CFO, so the net customer value exercise produces a credible metric that everyone understands and agrees on beforehand.

I learned this lesson the hard way early in my career when I ran a net customer value calculation for a growing company. The CEO gave me the assignment, but I created the formula without first getting any buy-in from the executive team, because I was a new employee and was eager to show my value.

Unfortunately, the calculation showed a decrease in net customer value despite a steady stream of new customers. Both the CEO and CFO refused to believe my conclusion. The CEO in particular got very angry with me, because he had just spent a lot of money implementing a new growth strategy.

The data turned out to be right. Those new customers spent far less than existing customers, and many did not return after their initial order. Meanwhile, chronically broken promises in product quality, order delivery, and customer service caused many high-value customers to leave. Within a year, the company ran into major cash flow issues, and the owners had to invest more money just to keep the organization afloat. A few years later, the company went out of business completely. Things might have been different if I'd made sure the CEO and CFO were on board with the calculation from the start and were willing to confront the truth about what it revealed.

The point of this calculation is to capture executives' attention so they view customer experience issues with a sense of urgency.

"We need to take people off the spreadsheet, and we want to give people a little agita, a little sick in the belly," says Bliss. "We've got to get our leaders pounding their hands on the table and saying, 'Why? Why? Why?! What happened?!'"

In the next chapter, we'll start to answer that question by discussing ways to ensure your company is keeping the promises it makes to its customers.

Chapter 5 Notes

1   Domino's Pizza 2008 Annual Report.

2   Stephanie Clifford, "Video Prank at Domino's Taints Brand," *The New York Times*, April 15, 2009.

3   Bruce Horovitz, "Domino's Pizza delivers change in core recipe," *USA Today*, December 16, 2009.

4   Michael Janofsky, "Domino's Ends Fast-Pizza Pledge After Big Award to Crash Victim," *The New York Times*, December 22, 1993.

5   "Domino's Launches Revolutionary Customer Tool: Pizza Tracker(TM)," Domino's Pizza press release, January 30, 2008.

6   Susan Berfield, "Domino's Atoned for its Crimes Against Pizza and Built a $9 Billion Empire," *Bloomberg Businessweek*, March 15, 2017.

7   Ibid.

8   "Domino's Pizza Pulling the Cheese," video posted on Facebook, July 13, 2010.

9   Matthew Dixon, Karen Freeman, and Nicholas Toman, "Stop Trying to Delight Your Customers," *Harvard Business Review*, July–August 2010.

10 Matthew Dixon, Nick Toman, and Rick Delisi, *The Effortless Experience*, Penguin Group, New York, 2013.

11 Jeff Toister, "The Best Way to Prevent Customers from Tweeting Complaints," *Inside Customer Service* blog, May 15, 2018.

12 Daniel Kahneman, *Thinking, Fast and Slow*, Farar, Straus, and Girous, New York, 2011.

Chapter 6
TAKING STEPS TO KEEP YOUR PROMISE

My heart was pounding.

I was scrambling up a mountain peak on a hot summer day. There was no trail to follow, so I had to rely on my GPS watch and signs left by previous hikers to navigate up the steep slope. I scanned the ground for rattlesnakes before each step and steadied myself several times to avoid slipping.

"Stay focused," I said to myself. "A lot could go wrong right now."

It was a solo hike, and there wasn't another person in sight. My phone had no signal, and the car was miles away. The remote trail was a long way from the nearest town, and I had driven for 20 minutes down a rutted dirt road to get to the trailhead.

The one bit of comfort was my Osprey backpack. I was wearing a Stratos model, and it felt light as a feather. The pack effortlessly clung to me as I clambered my way up the mountainside.

Pausing for a sip of water, I noticed a clever feature on the pack: a safety whistle integrated into the plastic buckle on the strap across my chest. "That might be really useful if I'm not careful," I thought.

You might think that experience would cause me to curtail future hikes. On the contrary, the journey to top of that isolated mountain made me want to go on even more adventures. The fresh air, breath-taking views, and quiet isolation all felt incredible.

The only problem was that my Stratos pack was too small for longer hikes where I wanted to bring multiple layers of clothing, extra food, or my camera. I needed a larger backpack for my next summit.

Choosing the right backpack can be a challenge. There's a dizzying array of brands and models on the market. Many look similar, but the differences become apparent on the trail. The way a pack fits, carries your gear, or even gives you an extra bit of confidence can all impact your hiking experience.

It helps to ask an expert for advice when making decisions like this.

The expert who helped me is Cris Hazzard, a.k.a. Hiking Guy. Hazzard leads guided hikes in Southern California and runs a website featuring detailed trail descriptions and gear recommendations. The website, HikingGuy.com, gets nearly 2 million visitors per year.

Hazzard is discerning when it comes to selecting gear to recommend on his website. Every item he features, from backpacks to hiking boots to GPS devices, is rigorously tested over many miles on the trail.

His go-to backpack brand is Osprey. It's the brand he uses personally and recommends to other hikers like me.

Hazzard has three basic criteria for selecting the backpacks he recommends. First, it has to fit well, since a good fit allows you to hike with ease. Second, the pack must have practical features to conveniently carry all your gear and allow you to quickly access items on the trail. And finally, a pack must also have a reputation for quality and its ability to withstand long miles in harsh elements.

"Osprey is really good at balancing features, pack weight, and durability," said Hazzard. He explained that every pack has to make certain trade-offs. For instance, an ultralight backpack might be easy to carry, but lack essential features or wear out easily. On the other hand, a backpack laden with all the features you could imagine might be too large or heavy.

Hazzard evaluates backpacks when manufacturers release new models. He considers the fit and features and reads customer reviews to see what other people are experiencing. He then purchases the most promising packs and tests each one out hiking.

One thing that consistently impresses him about Osprey is the quality. "I'm hiking hundreds and hundreds of miles per year," said Hazzard, "and I've never had anything fail."

Hazzard had three Osprey backpacks in his lineup when I sought his advice: a Stratos model like mine for shorter hikes, a Talon for longer day hikes or short overnight trips, and an Exos for multi-day camping excursions.

The Talon was exactly what I was looking for, and I bought it without considering any other brands. It's performed beautifully and has been a perfect addition to my lineup of backpacks.

Imagine if your company could build a reputation like Osprey's for keeping meaningful promises. Think about the impact on sales if experts recommended your products to millions of people and existing customers kept buying from you without giving the competition a single thought.

How to Ensure Your Promises are Kept

It's no accident that customer-focused companies keep their promises. Products and services are designed and rigorously tested with those promises in mind.

Osprey's brand promise is also its mission statement. It speaks directly to hikers who need a great pack: *We relentlessly innovate to ease your journey and inspire adventure.* Everything Osprey does is aligned around this brand promise.

According to Brian Mecham, Osprey's senior director of sales, this starts with the product design process. "Other pack companies might create three prototypes when developing new products," said Mecham. "At Osprey, we create anywhere from 10 to 18."

Features and design ideas are tested and refined over multiple iterations to ensure they will meet customers' needs. Mecham explained that other pack manufacturers outsource their prototype construction, but Osprey makes its own. "We have an in-house team that can do all the cutting and sewing on prototypes, so that gives us the ability to innovate much more."

This customer-focused design process results in unique features that make Osprey packs really stand out. The integrated safety whistle was something I hadn't noticed until I was on a remote trail, worrying about safety. My Osprey packs have a unique loop system that allows you to stow or retrieve your hiking poles without breaking stride. Backs tend to get sweaty when hiking on a warm day (gross!), and a pack that clings too tightly to your back will only add to the uncomfortable swampiness. My packs both have a special suspension system that allows air to flow between the pack and my back, which keeps everything cooler and drier.

Fit is particularly important to a hiker. A backpack should comfortably distribute the load so the pack doesn't feel too heavy, while also staying securely in place so the weight doesn't shift and make it hard to balance. "Osprey has a history of delivering innovation in the way the product fits," said Mecham. This is evident in the multiple straps and adjustment points that allow packs to be fitted to the wearer's individual body.

Recall that other companies profiled in this book design products and services that are focused on solving customer problems. Buc-ee's has built the largest, cleanest convenience store restrooms you've ever seen. Armstrong Garden Centers rigorously tests plants to ensure they will thrive in the local climate before selling them to customers. Zinus beds are designed to be incredibly easy for customers to assemble. GreatAmerica creates new financing products in response to equipment dealers' sales challenges. Domino's invented the Pizza Tracker™ to keep customers updated on the status of a delivery, so there would be no surprises about when the pizza would arrive.

But product design is just one part of keeping promises. Osprey invests a lot of time, money, and effort into helping customers choose the right backpack. There are many variables to consider, including the intended use, the carrying capacity, and even the customer's individual body. Some hikers, like Cris Hazzard and me, have multiple backpacks for different situations.

The Osprey website has a number of tools to help customers find the right pack. There's a Packfinder℠ tool that asks a series of questions to narrow down the options, such as gender, activity, trip length, packing style, and required features. The website also has a sizing guide customers can use to take their body measurements and determine the right pack size.

Of course, not every customer will search for a pack on the Osprey website. Many prefer to shop for backpacks in a store, where they can touch and feel different models and try on various options. This makes retailers who carry Osprey products an important part of the customer experience.

My wife, Sally, purchased my first Osprey pack for me as a gift after getting a recommendation from an associate at the outdoor gear retailer REI. A retail associate might suggest one brand over another, and they also spend time helping customers select the correct pack and adjusting it to fit properly.

Osprey provides a number of resources to help its retail partners deliver a customer experience that's aligned with the brand promise of *easing the customer's journey and inspiring adventure.* Its PEAK digital training program instructs retail associates on how to help customers select the right pack and ensure it fits correctly. National chains, such as REI, have access to in-person Osprey clinics where sales associates spend several days camping and using Osprey equipment, so they develop a more intimate knowledge of various packs and their features. Seasoned retail associates can become Osprey customer fit specialists, giving them access to additional training on how to properly fit a pack and specialized equipment to adjust a pack to customers' unique bodies.

Packs designed for extended backpacking trips can be especially challenging to fit. They tend to be larger and have more adjustment points than smaller packs. This makes it more difficult to help customers select the correct size and the right pack for their body type when they purchase online.

"The best fit is done in-store," said Mecham. "So we wanted to find a way to have customers purchase on Osprey.com and then go into a store."

In 2020, Osprey launched its Buy Online, Fit In-Store program. This allows customers to purchase a backpacking pack on the Osprey website and take it to a retail store to get the backpack professionally fitted. Participating retailers are given 15 percent of the sale as compensation for assisting customers.[1]

A well-trained retail associate can ensure customers get the best fit or exchange their purchase for a more suitable pack if the one they purchased isn't quite right. Customers are also likely to make additional purchases while in the store, which further strengthens the value Osprey provides to retailers.

It's essential to identify and support third parties that play a critical role in keeping your experience promises. This includes retailers, franchise operators, delivery companies, outsourced contact centers, and other partners. The more these partners are aligned with your experience promises, the more likely those promises are to be kept.

The customer experience doesn't end once a customer purchases your product. Customers often need additional support to learn how to use all of a product's features or solve minor problems. Where people might have contacted a customer service department in the past, many now prefer to search online for resources to solve issues on their own. These resources can take the form of how-to guides, instructional manuals, explainer videos, or even online discussion boards.

For example, many Osprey packs come with an array of unusual loops, straps, and pockets. The company produces helpful explainer videos to demonstrate these features and explain how they work. One video revealed that my Osprey Stratos pack has a loop and tie system designed to secure an ice axe, which now has me seriously thinking about a winter mountain climbing adventure.

Even the best-made products eventually wear out. That's why Osprey offers an industry-leading warranty on its packs called the All Mighty Guarantee. The company will repair or replace any Osprey pack that has a defect or gets damaged, no matter how old.

Osprey's quest to ease its customers' journeys inspired the company to take its guarantee a step further. It sets up an onsite repair shop at the Appalachian Trail Days Festival. The festival is an annual gathering in Damascus, Virginia, for hikers and supporters of the nearly 2,200-mile Appalachian Trail that runs from Georgia to Maine. Osprey offers customers free repairs and pack adjustments to help them continue their hike.

"Us being here is a necessity," said Osprey repair manager Andrew Baxley. "We're out here to be a presence and to get their packs back on the road, so they can continue hiking. Because it's a long trail, and they need to get to Maine.[2]"

Keeping customer promises is all about *intention*. Promises are made with the *intention* of keeping them. Products, services, and processes are *intentionally* designed to ensure that happens.

This applies to personal promises as well—or at least, it should. But many customer service professionals instinctively make promises to help customers feel better in the moment, without any specific intention to ensure the promise is kept.

For example, let's say you're helping a customer resolve an issue. You've identified the solution and think it will take just a little bit of time to implement. There's a natural urge to promise a fast resolution to help the customer feel relief, so customer service reps often tell the customer, "I'll take care of it right away."

Unfortunately, as we discussed in Chapter 4, the term "right away" is vague and unclear. The customer might be disappointed if their understanding is different than yours. A better approach is to use clear language and give the customer a specific time when you'll respond.

Giving a specific time often requires us to stop and think through the situation. We must consider how long it took to complete similar tasks in the past. It's also important to account for any variables that might slow us down, such as the availability of coworkers to assist us or interruptions from other customers.

One more variable to consider is optimism. Even thoughtful service professionals are often too optimistic when giving customers an estimated response time. They think they can get something done in an hour if everything goes right, so they promise the customer one hour because that brings the customer relief in the moment.

What if something goes wrong? The customer will be disappointed if we fail to keep our promise.

A better approach is to give yourself some wiggle room when making promises. When giving a customer an estimated completion time, it's better to give a worst-case estimate. Try to account for variables that might slow you down, and think of the latest you would get something done. So if the best-case scenario is solving the customer's problem in one hour, but the worst-case is three hours, then give the customer the worst-case estimate.

Customers typically agree to the worst-case scenario as long as it's still reasonable. Now you have three hours to complete the task, instead of one, which gives you some breathing room if something goes wrong.

This doesn't mean you should rest easy. Some customer service professionals make the mistake of relaxing and taking it slow after negotiating more time than they think they need. This extra time is a safety net and should only be used if absolutely necessary. Any deliberate slowdown will hurt you if something unexpected comes up as you near the deadline.

A better approach is to state the worst-case scenario, and then aim for the best-case scenario. Resolving the issue within one hour allows you to exceed expectations. Even a two-hour response time is better than the three you and the customer agreed upon in this scenario.

The important thing is to keep your promise.

What Happens if You Aren't Intentional About Keeping Promises

In April 2017, an episode of the popular adult cartoon show, *Rick and Morty*, presented McDonald's with a unique marketing opportunity. The episode's plot revolved around a character searching for McDonald's Szechuan sauce, a limited-edition condiment that was offered with Chicken McNuggets® for a short time in 1998 as part of a promotion for the Disney movie *Mulan*.

Rick and Morty fans began lobbying McDonald's to bring back the Szechuan sauce. More than 38,000 people signed an online petition asking for it. McDonald's got in on the fun and sent a bottle of the sauce to Justin Roiland, one of the show's creators.

The story generated positive publicity, so McDonald's tried to take it a step further. The company announced it would bring back limited quantities of the Szechuan sauce for one day only at participating locations across the United States.

The terms "limited quantities" and "participating locations" are used to protect organizations from making firm promises. They're intended to avoid a legal guarantee that supplies won't run out, or that every location will have some. Yet that fine print is lost on customers who see a promise and expect it to be fulfilled. On the day of the promotion, *Rick and Morty* fans lined up in droves at McDonald's locations throughout the country, expecting to get their hands on the sauce.

Unfortunately, McDonald's failed to take the steps necessary to deliver the promised Szechuan sauce to legions of fans. Some stores received as few as 20 packets of sauce and quickly ran out. Others never received any sauce at all.

Hundreds of angry customers gathered outside multiple McDonald's locations to demand Szechuan sauce. In one viral video, a customer is seen jumping on the counter and yelling about sauce while stunned employees and customers look on. Police were called to help contain the crowds at many locations. Complaints trended on social media.[3]

What began as a fun marketing stunt failed miserably, because McDonald's wasn't intentional about keeping its promise. It didn't anticipate demand and failed to ensure that stores were adequately supplied.

The McDonald's story is extreme, but it's hardly unusual. Products fail, services falter, and experiences fall short of expectations. How many times have these things happened to you?

★ A restaurant got your order wrong.

★ A store wouldn't honor an advertised promotion.

★ A salesperson lied or exaggerated to sell you something.

★ A technician arrived late, or didn't arrive at all.

★ A new product was defective.

★ A mechanic recommended expensive repairs your car didn't need.

★ A customer service rep promised to call you back, but didn't.

My guess is most, if not all, of these things have happened to you—probably more than once. Companies everywhere routinely disappoint customers with broken promises.

Lack of alignment is often to blame. Companies are organized into departmental fiefdoms, with each group having separate goals. Marketing is measured by the number of leads it generates. Sales is judged by the number of new customers it acquires. Operations is focused on meeting production and shipping quotas. Customer service is evaluated by how efficiently it handles complaints.

One electronics company marketed a hub that allowed customers to connect multiple peripherals to a computer, such as monitors, speakers, webcams, printers, and other devices. The hub was designed to be compatible with any Mac or PC running the latest operating system, but a problem arose when Apple launched its latest MacBook. The hub didn't work with the new computer.

Apple and other resellers were given this information and updated their websites accordingly. Unfortunately, several of the company's internal departments didn't get the message. The company's website continued to claim it would run on any Mac with a current operating system. The update also didn't make it to technical support, so support agents tried in vain to troubleshoot the issue without realizing it couldn't be solved. That led to longer customer wait times, frustrated customers, and a spike in returned products.

Promises are hard to keep if you aren't intentional about keeping them. Service failures are inevitable when a marketing team launches a promotion without first ironing out the details, or product updates are haphazardly communicated. Actions must be aligned around the promises a brand, product, or individual employee makes to customers.

The customer-focused companies you've met so far in this book succeed by being intentional where their competitors routinely fail.

Exercise: Design a Process to Keep Your Promise

PDCA is a reliable tool that can help you design a new process or modify an existing one to ensure your promises are kept. PDCA is an acronym that outlines four stages:

1. Plan

2. Do

3. Check

4. Adjust

This tool can be very sophisticated, with multiple levels, variations, and aspects, but I prefer to keep it high level for the purposes of this book.

If you'd like a more comprehensive guide to using PDCA and other problem-solving tools, I recommend *The Problem-Solver's Toolkit*, by Elisabeth Swan and Tracy O'Rourke. It's an excellent book full of practical tools, guides, and examples.

For this exercise, let's go back to the workbook we've been using to complete the exercises at the end of each chapter and use PDCA to outline a process to keep your promise. (You can download the workbook, if you haven't already, at guaranteedexperience.com/workbook.)

Plan

Imagine you're going on a journey. The first thing you need to know is your destination. A destination is essential to planning your route or using your GPS navigation system to guide you. You'll know what essential items to bring with you, such as a jacket if you're going to a cold destination, or sunscreen if your destination is warm and sunny. Visualizing your journey can also help you anticipate what obstacles you might encounter along the way.

Keeping promises works like planning a journey. It starts by thinking of the promise you want to deliver, and then working backwards to create your plan. This first step is essential whether you're designing something new or modifying an existing product or process.

I find it helpful to phrase the promise as a question. Here are some examples from promises we've encountered so far:

★ Buc-ee's: How can we offer customers the cleanest restrooms?

★ Armstrong: How can we help people garden without guesswork?

★ Zinus: How can we deliver mattresses, bed frames, and couches to our customer's door?

★ GreatAmerica: How can we help equipment dealers improve sales with financing?

★ Domino's: How can we deliver hot, delicious pizza?

★ Osprey: How can we ease our customers' journeys and inspire adventure?

Each of these questions can generate endless ideas for keeping the promise. Try asking a similar question. "How can we keep our promise?" (Or, if it's a personal promise, "How can I keep my promise?")

This question can help you visualize a process for keeping your promise. Write out the steps involved, or create a diagram, flowchart, or other tool that includes who's responsible for doing what and when. Recording your plan makes it easier to follow and remember.

There are two perspectives that should always be considered when creating your plan.

First, who are the people who will be responsible for keeping the promise? Whenever possible, stakeholders from these groups should be involved in the planning process. Stakeholders might include:

★ Product designers

★ Marketing

★ Sales

★ Operations

★ Customer support

★ Third-party partners

Your customers' perspectives are also an important part of the planning process. During brainstorming sessions, it's easy to lose sight of *why* you're generating ideas, or what problem you're trying to solve. Customer feedback from interactions, focus groups, surveys, and other sources can be invaluable.

Here's an example from The Overlook, the vacation rental cabin I mentioned in Chapter 3. Our brand promise is *Welcome to your mountain retreat*, because we want it to be a place where guests can relax and enjoy the mountains.

My wife, Sally, and I had a lot of ideas when we first purchased the cabin, but we made sure we shared them with our property manager before making any big decisions. That's because our property manager was responsible for marketing and maintaining the cabin. She had a lot of valuable input on what ideas would work and which would not.

The cabin was already a vacation rental property when we purchased it, so we reviewed feedback from previous guests. We also interviewed people we knew who frequently rented other cabins in the area to learn more about what guests expected and what they generally liked and disliked about various rentals. We spent several nights at the cabin before renting it so we could experience it ourselves. All these insights helped us understand what supplies we needed, what furnishings needed updating or repairing, and what amenities might be missing.

Do

The next step in the PDCA model is to implement your plan on a trial basis. This gives you the opportunity to test it before you conduct a large-scale rollout.

Check

Evaluate the results of your trial run and verify whether your promises were consistently kept. Get feedback from your customers. You'll usually find opportunities for improvement.

Adjust

Use data from your trial run to make adjustments. This gives you a chance to strengthen your promise-keeping process before conducting a widespread rollout.

You can repeat the PDCA process as needed until you have a high degree of confidence your promises will be kept. Recall that Osprey makes as many as 18 prototypes of new backpacks before releasing a new model. That might seem like a lot of iterations, but the end result is a backpack that outperforms the competition.

Using this exercise, you'll create a process that ensures your promises are kept reliably. It can take a lot of work to get things right, but the payoff comes when you attract and retain more customers than your competition—because people know they can count on you to keep your word.

Chapter 6 Notes

1   Kristin Hostetter, "New Osprey program drives traffic and revenue to retailers," *SNEWS*, May 7, 2020.

2   Osprey website, accessed August 5, 2020, https://www.osprey.com/us/en/customer-support/all-mighty-guarantee.

3   Michael Cavna and Maura Judkis, "McDonald's botched its 'Rick and Morty' Szechuan sauce stunt, and fans are not happy," *The Washington Post*, October 9, 2017.

Chapter 7

MONITORING THE CUSTOMER EXPERIENCE

Daniel Pascoe has never owned a car.

That might seem inconceivable to many people, but a car isn't necessary if you live in a city that has reliable public transportation—like Portland, Oregon. Portland's transportation system is run by TriMet, which provides bus, light rail, and commuter rail service.

Pascoe uses the bus to get to work and visit other parts of town. He occasionally uses TriMet's MAX light rail. "The MAX is really convenient when you're going to the airport," he explained. "It takes you right into the terminal."

Customers like Pascoe are trying to solve a transportation problem. They need to get from one place to another, and TriMet makes two fundamental promises to help them. The first is the published routes, which assure passengers they can get from their starting point to their destination. The second is the schedule, which promises to get passengers there by a certain time.

For Pascoe, TriMet's ability to consistently keep those promises makes him a fan of the service. He knows he can depend on TriMet to get him to work, or wherever else he wants to go, on time. "Reliability is a positive that TriMet is known for."

Consistently keeping those promises isn't easy. TriMet provides approximately 100 million passenger rides per year and covers a geographical region spanning 533 square miles. Traffic jams, inclement weather, construction, the occasional mechanical failure, and the sheer size of the system make it difficult to keep everything running on time.

One way TriMet inspires confidence is by sharing real-time arrival and departure information. This information allows passengers to make adjustments if their particular bus or train is running ahead of or behind schedule.

Pascoe stays updated via text. "There is a phone number posted at every bus stop. You just text the stop ID to that phone number and get an update on the next arrival." The updates usually come within seconds and are generally very accurate. He looks for arrival information when he's heading to or from work, so he knows if he needs to leave immediately to catch an arriving bus or if he has a little extra time.

Lucia McArdle is another Portland-area resident who's a fan of TriMet. "It's been my primary method of transportation," McArdle explained. Like Pascoe, McArdle doesn't own a car and relies on the bus to get to work. Compared to other transportation options, such as owning a car or using ride-sharing services like Uber, "TriMet is pretty convenient and a lot cheaper."

McArdle stays updated on arrival and departure times with Moovit, a third-party app that provides schedules, navigation, maps, and real-time updates. Relying on data provided by TriMet, the app tells her when the next bus is arriving at a particular stop. McArdle has found it to be accurate and timely. "I think TriMet is doing a really good job of updating third parties."

Occasional delays are inevitable no matter what form of transportation you choose. Both Pascoe and McArdle have had experiences where their bus was delayed. This is when it's especially helpful to have access to real-time updates to know when the next bus is coming.

The wait can be much longer for buses serving outlying areas, so having accurate information lets riders decide what to do next. Someone commuting to work, for example, might have to call ahead to let their boss know they're going to be late, find an alternate route, or even use a ride-sharing service to get to work on time if the delay will be too long. Both Pascoe and McArdle agreed that it was better to have accurate information about their transportation options than to wonder whether or not they'll be able to get to work on time.

Occasionally, a mechanical problem, emergency road construction, or some other unexpected issue causes a bus or train to stop. This is where TriMet really shines.

I experienced TriMet's responsiveness while riding the MAX light rail to the airport. The train had just pulled into a station when the operator announced a delay. Passengers exchanged worried looks as they wondered if they'd still be able to catch their flight. One family of four was already cutting it close to their flight's departure time, and they grew increasingly agitated with each passing minute.

A few minutes later, the operator announced that the train would not continue due to a problem on the track, and buses would be provided to shuttle passengers to another station where they could rejoin the light rail. People became even more nervous about their flights, unsure of when the shuttle buses would arrive or how much longer it would take to get to the airport.

The buses arrived quickly despite everyone's fears. We were efficiently transported to another station where a train was waiting to take us the rest of the way to the airport. The total delay was only about 30 minutes, and even the panicked family made it in time to catch their flight.

TriMet wins fans like Pascoe, McArdle, and me by keeping its promises to get passengers to a particular place by a certain time. This is an incredibly difficult challenge with multiple bus routes and rail lines spanning a wide geographical region. What really helps TriMet stand out is its ability to constantly monitor the customer experience and make adjustments before small problems become broken promises.

How to Monitor the Customer Experience for Broken Promises

One of the most important aspects of a Guaranteed Customer Experience is a system to ensure promises are being kept.

TriMet has something called the Operations Command Center to monitor its transportation network and provide real-time information and updates to operators, passengers, and other critical stakeholders. Video screens line the walls. Some show live camera feeds from various points along bus routes and rail lines, while others are continuously updated with important data. Employees are in contact with bus and train operators, repair crews, and other relevant personnel.

The command center is staffed 24 hours per day, seven days a week, with as many as 30 employees at any given time. The center is divided into three teams, with each team monitoring their section of Portland's geographical region. Employees keep an eye on buses, light rail lines, and trains to ensure they're running on time and to detect problems as quickly as they happen.

Jon Bell is TriMet's senior manager of customer experience. He explained that the command center employees are charged with helping TriMet keep its brand promise: *We connect people with their community.*

"We're not buses and trains," said Bell. "We're connecting people to life. We are truly the thread of the community, connecting people to jobs, school, family, and friends."

Bell understands that thousands of passengers rely on TriMet to be on time. "The moment you break that promise, that is a moment of truth." People won't trust TriMet if it's not reliable.

Employees in the Operations Command Center spring into action when an issue is detected and there's a danger that a bus or train might be delayed. They share alerts about accidents, construction, traffic congestion, and other problems. Command center employees work with bus and train operations to coordinate a solution to keep passengers moving while providing updated information on the status.

Passengers have a wide range of options for staying updated on transit schedules. The TriMet website features trip-planning tools, real-time arrival information for each route and station, and service alerts. Passengers can sign up to get alerts via email or text. Route stops have a unique ID that passengers use to get arrival information via text, while busier stops also have electronic display boards listing the expected arrival time of incoming buses or trains. Critical updates are provided on social media, and passengers can call TriMet to get arrival times or assistance planning a trip. There are also third-party apps, like Moovit, that share updated information.

Customer-focused organizations like TriMet create robust systems to monitor customer experience and sound alarms when promises might be broken. While many of these systems might appear insanely complicated, they're based on two simple questions:

1. What promises are we making?

2. How do we know we're keeping our promises?

Monitoring for broken promises allows you to identify problems and fix them quickly. Some problems are easy to see. For example, one client promising fast service implemented a simple visual system at their customer service desk. Employees were trained to contact a colleague or supervisor for additional help whenever they saw waiting customers standing next to a particular sign posted on the wall. To customers, the sign was an innocuous display of helpful information, but to employees it was a visual cue that the line had gotten too long and they were in danger of breaking their promise of fast service.

Other promises require data to monitor and detect problems. For example, email remains a popular channel for customers to contact companies. Research conducted by my company reveals that customers expect increasingly fast responses, and organizations should respond to customer emails within one hour.[1] Many customer service teams track their email response time, so they know whether or not they're meeting this standard. The manager then has the ability to detect issues with their teams' response time.

Some companies, like Amazon, use automation to search data for signs of a potential problem. When a customer places an order, the items are picked from warehouse shelves and packed into a box. The box is then routed through a special machine that weighs the package and compares the actual weight to the expected weight of the shipment. Any discrepancy is a signal that the box likely has a missing or incorrect item. If the weights don't match, the box is automatically pushed off the shipping line into a quality control station for an employee to inspect.

Companies often collect customer experience data but may not be using it proactively to identify, track, and solve broken promises. Here are just a few places where you can look to find signs of broken promises:

★ Account cancellations

★ Product return rates

★ Delivery tracking records

★ Customer service contacts

★ Social media mentions

★ Online reviews

★ Customer service surveys

One of the most overlooked opportunities to detect broken promises is to ask frontline employees for feedback. They have frequent interactions with customers and can easily describe the types of complaints they hear most often. Asking employees to share those complaints will help managers start a list of issues to investigate.

Another way to monitor for broken promises is to be your own customer. Each week, I send out an email called the *Customer Service*

Tip of the Week to thousands of subscribers. (You can subscribe for free at toistersolutions.com/tips.) There are occasionally errors in the email, such as a typo or a broken link, that slip through despite a rigorous testing process. As a final validation, I subscribe to my own email, so I can see what time it arrives in my inbox and see the email from a subscriber's perspective. When there's an error that will impact the customer experience, such as a broken web link, I can quickly fix the problem and alert subscribers before most people ever notice there's an issue.

Elite leaders are adept at using the tiniest of clues to spot early warning signs of a broken promise. I call this hunting icebergs. An iceberg is a problem that appears small and manageable on the surface but is actually the tip of a much larger and dangerous issue that remains unseen.

A client once discovered a $50,000 billing problem after fielding a single customer complaint. The customer had encountered a billing issue that theoretically couldn't happen in the company's billing system. Since the error did in fact occur, the manager sought out the root cause and discovered a software glitch that only affected a few customers in unusual situations. While the problem was rare, it happened often enough that it cost the company $50,000 in lost revenue per year. The software was quickly fixed with just a few lines of code.

Icebergs can usually be investigated by doing what's called a "gemba walk." This involves going to where the work is done and observing it first-hand. It requires you to approach the situation with an open mind and ask questions to gain a better understanding of how people do the work and why they do it the way they do.[2]

An airline customer service director noticed his contact center was fielding a lot of calls from passengers struggling to use the airline's self check-in kiosks at the airport. The questions seemed very basic, and the director wasn't sure why people struggled. So he went to a nearby airport and spent time helping passengers check in at the kiosks to better understand the challenges passengers experienced.

What he observed was illuminating. The on-screen instructions were confusing, especially to someone who was an infrequent traveler. There were employees stationed nearby to help passengers, but there were too few to handle the volume of passenger questions. The customer service director also realized his contact center agents didn't have the most accurate information about how the self check-in process actually worked.

The observations from the director's gemba walk helped improve the customer experience and prevent broken promises. The self check-in process was updated to make it easier and more intuitive. Airport employees were given better training on how to assist customers quickly. And contact center agents were given more accurate information about the check-in process so they could better help customers who got stuck.

Individual employees should also monitor the promises they make. It's risky to assume that work has been done or a problem handled without verification. For instance, when a client asks me to email a document, I look for a return email acknowledging the document was received. I've learned that emails sometimes get stuck in spam folders or blocked by the client's corporate email servers. This might cause the client to think I broke my promise and forgot to send the document.

If I don't get an acknowledgement within a reasonable amount of time (usually one business day), I'll follow up. On most occasions, they've received my email, but it's amazing how many times they haven't. That short follow-up message serves as a signal that I haven't forgotten, and also as a subtle message that I kept my promise. This prevents clients from being upset with me, and many appreciate the follow-up.

The sooner a broken promise is detected, the better.

A customer who arranges time off work to meet a repair technician would rather hear the night before that the technician will be delayed, instead of discovering they'll be late after the promised arrival time has come and gone. Alerting the customer to a possible delay the night before gives them options, such as rescheduling the repair for a more convenient time. The customer's time is wasted if they don't learn about the delay until after the technician's arrival window has passed.

My wife, Sally, and I have an Ecobee smart thermostat installed at The Overlook, our vacation rental property. The thermostat is connected to the internet, so we can monitor the cabin's temperature remotely. The system even sends us alerts when there appears to be an issue with our heating or air conditioning system.

On one very hot day, we received an automated alert that The Overlook's air conditioner had been running for several hours, but the cabin wasn't cooling down. We contacted our property manager, who in turn contacted our guests to check on the issue. They were outside enjoying the cabin's deck and lounging in the spa, blissfully unaware that the cabin was becoming uncomfortably warm inside. Fortunately, we were able to find a solution to the intense heat and get the system working again before it negatively impacted our guests' experience.

A company that makes manufacturing equipment has a robust inspection process for every machine it builds. The machines are all large, complicated, and sell for hundreds of thousands of dollars, so the stakes are high each time it ships an order to a customer. The machines are inspected at the factory using a highly-choreographed routine, and then inspected and tested again at the customer's site by the installers. This process ensures that problems are detected and rectified before they have a negative impact on the customer.

Some broken promises can be anticipated before a problem ever occurs. My wife and I hired a mobile auto detailing company to come to our home and detail our two vehicles. The company's owner called the night before our scheduled appointment and explained that rain was forecast during our appointment time. He offered to keep the original appointment or reschedule it for the following day, when the weather was expected to be better. A detailing service promises a clean, beautiful car, and the owner averted the weather from ruining that promise by anticipating the issue and providing a proactive solution.

This has become the communication philosophy for TriMet in recent years. The organization has shifted its focus from emphasizing on-time arrivals to providing passengers with accurate information to help them better plan their trips. Too many variables made it difficult to consistently keep the same schedule every day. Bell and his colleagues also realized that maintaining a high percentage of on-time arrivals wasn't what passengers cared about the most. "You have to choose what's important to you, and make sure that's what's important to the customer."

What's truly important to passengers is knowing the status of any particular trip. A 95 percent on-time record won't help passengers if the specific bus they were hoping to catch that day is running late. Riders like Daniel Pascoe and Lucia McArdle have confidence that TriMet provides accurate and updated information to help them arrive on time. Both told me that minor delays generally aren't a big problem, so long as they remain informed.

This is where they give TriMet high marks for providing helpful information and proactive solutions to most problems. As McArdle told me, "If something happens to the number eight bus, there's usually another one just a few minutes behind it, so it's not a big deal."

In the rare instances when a longer delay occurs, TriMet is ready. Recall that the light rail train I was riding to the airport was unexpectedly stopped due to an issue farther down the track. What could have been a huge problem ended up being just a 30-minute delay, and we all arrived at the airport in time to catch our flights.

What Happens If You Don't Monitor the Customer Experience

There was a long line of angry customers waiting to speak to a customer service representative. The line spilled out of the lobby into the street outside, where the throng of upset people continued to swell.

Most customers wanted refunds. The company had failed to keep many of its promises, and people felt they deserved their money back. The stone-faced customer service representatives steadfastly refused, quoting company policy and nodding towards the glowering supervisor who paced behind them.

A sobbing mother pushed her way inside the lobby and pleaded for help finding her lost child. The two had become separated in the growing crowd, and she was desperate. A bad day was getting worse.

I was just seven years old and had looked forward to a fun outing with my mom, dad, aunt, and uncle. Now we were in line with the rest of the angry customers, trying to get a refund and salvage a terrible day. When it was our turn, the employee initially refused our request. My mom wouldn't take no for an answer, so a supervisor stepped in. After she still wouldn't take no for an answer, we were escorted to a back room where a manager attempted to negotiate by offering a discount. My mom wouldn't budge, and the manager finally relented and refunded our money.

The manager then had an employee escort us out through a back entrance so we wouldn't be seen. My uncle observed that there might be a riot if the other angry customers learned we got a refund.

You might be wondering where this terrible scene unfolded. It was none other than the self-proclaimed *Happiest Place on Earth*. The angry crowd of customers, the backroom negotiations, and that sobbing mother are my most lasting childhood memories of Disneyland.

Disneyland failed to monitor the number of guests entering the park that day. A steady stream of visitors kept coming through the gates and soon filled the park beyond capacity. The shortest line for a ride stretched over two hours. Crowds of people were so thick that moving anywhere around the park required you to shuffle and jostle your way forward at a snail's pace. My uncle put me on his shoulders to protect me from all the pushing and shoving.

This experience was the antithesis of what Disneyland promises to its guests. It had all the right ingredients to promise a magical experience—the rides, the shows and attractions, the costumed characters ready to greet children—but the sheer number of customers overwhelmed the system. Thousands of guests were disappointed that day, and I can only hope that mother quickly found her lost child.

Disneyland's opening day in 1955 was also marred by over-crowding. It was supposed to be an invitation-only preview for the press and invited guests, but more than double the expected attendance arrived.

Walt Disney, known for his intense focus on details, had pushed so hard to get the park open in time for the press day that many details were uncharacteristically overlooked. Guests got wet paint on their clothes, and women in high heels found their shoes stuck in soft asphalt. Food quickly ran out. Rides broke down. There were long lines at the restrooms.[3]

Disney has weathered multiple overcrowding incidents over the years because it has learned from them. Crowds still present a challenge at the company's theme parks, but procedures have greatly improved. Lines move more efficiently, and Disney now provides eerily accurate wait time estimates. Ride malfunctions are quickly communicated and addressed. Guests can download an app providing up-to-the-minute wait times and operating status of rides and attractions. Disney's theme parks even close to new guests once they hit capacity.[4]

It was a few years after my terrible experience before I went back to Disneyland. I grew up in Southern California, close enough to make a day trip to the theme park, but my parents refused to go. It wasn't until another uncle, Dennis, came to visit and offered to take me that I had another chance. This time, there were virtually no crowds at all, and we walked right onto many of the most popular rides without ever waiting in line. It was an amazing experience that reclaimed the magic of visiting a Disney park, and I remain a fan to this day.

The customer experience erodes quickly when companies fail to monitor it, or if they fail to fix problems once they're detected. Some, like Disney, learn from mistakes and create better systems and processes to detect and avoid broken promises before they lose too many customers. Other organizations are slow to react, if they react at all, and suffer the consequences.

In his book *How the Mighty Fall*, Jim Collins examined the reasons why great companies fail. This includes organizations once considered leaders in their industries that all suffered precipitous declines, such as Circuit City, Motorola, and Zenith. One of the more surprising discoveries is that companies can be several steps down the path towards failure before it becomes obvious in the company's financial results. By then, these companies often have what Collins described as a "culture of denial," where leadership teams focus on insulating themselves from the facts instead of searching for ways to improve.[5]

A culture of denial allows even obvious issues to go undetected. One customer service leader told me his team was overwhelmed with customer complaints after the company had a string of broken promises. Executives denied his request to hire more people while also refusing to address the source of the problems. The unusually large number of complaints led to longer response times and even unhappier customers.

These were all signs of chronic issues, which soon began to eat into revenue as fed up customers took their business to competitors. The customer service leader eventually lost his job as executives desperately tried to cut costs.

Some executives believe they're adequately monitoring customer experience with surveys. Unfortunately, survey programs tend to be rife with problems. Many executives have confidentially admitted to me that they don't actively use the surveys to identify issues and improve customer experience. Their primary objective is to generate a score that makes the company look good to investors and other key stakeholders.

Companies often resort to manipulative surveys that are intentionally designed to produce higher scores. The way a question is worded, how a rating scale is designed, or even how a survey is presented, can all influence customers' scores. A study by the customer feedback consulting firm Interaction Metrics found that 68 percent of surveys offered at the bottom of purchase receipts were "total garbage," meaning the surveys were so deeply flawed that they revealed little, if any, useful information.[6]

Employees are frequently incentivized to engage in manipulation. They're given bonuses for good survey scores or risk some form of punishment if their scores are too low. This has caused rampant survey begging, where employees plead with customers to give them a good score, often in exchange for a small discount or some other favor. Employees are sometimes able to control who gets offered a survey, so they only give surveys to customers who appear to be happy.

Another challenge is that the survey itself is part of the customer experience. Asking a customer to answer a few questions is essentially asking them to do your business a favor. Companies often make surveys an unpleasant experience by making them difficult to access and then overloading them with unnecessary questions that waste customers' time. Meanwhile, customers experience survey fatigue when every other business asks them to do the same thing.

One restaurant chain offered a survey on its dining receipt that contained more than 50 questions spread out over 39 different screens. The survey lacked a mobile-friendly version, so customers either had to stare at tiny text on their phones or access the survey on a computer. It asked pointless questions that could have been answered via the restaurant's point-of-sale computer system, such as the location they visited, the date they dined there, and the time of day when they arrived.

Surveys can be powerful experience-monitoring tools, but they should be used to help identify potential problems, not needlessly annoy your customers or contribute to the culture of denial that Jim Collins warned about.

Even positive surveys can help you identify opportunities for improvement. On one client's survey project, I discovered negative comments in five percent of survey responses where customers gave the highest rating. These customers were very happy, but they still had constructive feedback to share.

Your customers are monitoring their experience even if you aren't. An express delivery company tried to compete with more established services like UPS and FedEx. It initially won many new clients by promising lower prices, but the experience was incredibly uneven. Shipments were often delayed or even damaged, and the company was slow to respond to complaints.

People began to take notice. They complained to the companies using the delivery service to ship their products. Many of those companies, worried about the impact on their own reputation, cancelled their contracts and went back to UPS or FedEx. Customers also posted hundreds of negative online reviews on sites like Yelp, where the delivery company's one-star rating serves as a clear warning sign to potential prospects that they should stay away.

The company's executives had multiple data points that could have alerted them to trouble. The poor delivery record, large number of damage claims, and extensive service complaints should all have sounded warning bells. The negative online reviews provided another glimpse into customer sentiment that went unheeded. The result of the executives' inaction was a significant loss of customers and a bad reputation that made it more difficult to acquire new ones.

Exercise: Create an Experience Monitoring System

An experience monitoring system is an essential part of delivering a Guaranteed Customer Experience. It will help you keep your promises and avoid service failures. And if something does go wrong, you can quickly detect and fix the issue.

There's a worksheet to guide you through the steps below in the downloadable workbook at guaranteedexperience.com/workbook.

To create an experience monitoring system, start by answering the two questions from earlier in this chapter:

1. What promises are we making?

2. How do we know we're keeping our promises?

You need data to determine if you're keeping your promises. It's also helpful to know how frequently promises are broken. As a reminder, here are a few places where you can find data on broken promises:

★ Account cancellations

★ Product return rates

★ Delivery tracking records

★ Customer service contacts

★ Social media mentions

★ Online reviews

★ Customer service surveys

★ Feedback from employees

★ Quality inspections

Look for ways to detect problems early. Better yet, see if you can spot problems before customers are affected. TriMet monitors its network in real-time. A manufacturer conducts detailed inspections to ensure its machines are defect-free before they're shipped to a customer. Ecobee sends automated alerts when an air conditioner isn't performing properly.

It helps to start simple. Few organizations need large, sophisticated command centers to monitor their services like TriMet has. Many promises can be easily monitored with minimal technology and few, if any, additional personnel.

Hotel housekeeping departments provide an example of a simple yet robust monitoring system. One promise every hotel makes to its guests is a clean room, and the housekeeping department is responsible for fulfilling that promise.

This promise is monitored in a number of ways. Housekeepers report when a room has been cleaned, so front desk associates know they can check guests into the room. A room sometimes needs extra cleaning or has some damage that needs to be repaired, so housekeepers delay reporting until the unexpected issue has been fixed. Supervisors regularly inspect a sample of cleaned rooms and observe housekeepers at work to verify they're doing their jobs correctly.

Despite all those efforts, a few hotel guests might still find cleanliness issues when they check into their room. Some complain, typically to the hotel's front desk, and those complaints are routed to the housekeeping department. Many hotels also survey their guests upon departure, and surveys that call out cleanliness issues can be flagged for additional investigation.

It helps to track issues over time so you can identify larger trends. A one-time failure could be the result of a simple mistake, but repeated failures are likely a sign of a systemic problem.

One hotel experienced chronic complaints about room cleanliness. An investigation revealed that housekeepers weren't following established cleaning procedures. The department lacked the needed cleaning supplies to properly clean rooms, so housekeepers had been taking shortcuts. The cleanliness issue was quickly solved when the correct supplies were ordered and a better system was implemented to ensure the needed supplies were re-ordered when inventory was low.

In some cases, you might find it necessary to add new monitoring systems if your existing actions aren't enough to detect problems and alert you to trouble. For example, Sally and I have a checklist we use to perform regular inspections and preventative maintenance tasks at The Overlook. We often discover new issues we haven't encountered before, such as a crack in the fireplace that needed repair. Once the problem has been addressed, it gets added to the inspection checklist, so we can continue to monitor our cabin for recurring issues.

There are endless ways to create an experience monitoring system. The simplest is to focus on answering the question, "How do we know we're keeping our promises?" Keeping this question top of mind will help you build effective habits for avoiding customer disappointment.

Chapter 7 Notes

1   Jeff Toister, "How quickly should you respond to email?" *Inside Customer Service* blog, April 7, 2020.

2   The term gemba (or genba) is a Japanese word that means "the actual place." It's a principle closely associated with lean manufacturing, but I've always found it to be a great way to diagnose service failures.

3   Richard Snow, "Disneyland Hasn't Always Been the Happiest Place on Earth," *Scribner*, December 12, 2019.

4   Hugo Martin, "Disneyland hits capacity, temporarily stops selling tickets," *Los Angeles Times*, December 27, 2019.

5   Jim Collins, *How the Mighty Fall*, Harper Collins, New York, 2009.

6   Interaction Metrics, "2016 Findings Report, The State of POP Retail Surveys."

PART IV: RECOVERY

What will you do if you don't keep your promise?

Chapter 8
WHY YOU NEED A SERVICE RECOVERY PLAN

Chelsea Howell was experiencing a string of bad luck.

First she was laid off from her job. A short while later, she was involved in a minor traffic accident that damaged her car. An insurance claim covered the repairs, but a few days after getting her car back, she noticed a tire pressure warning light.

Sure enough, one of the tires was leaking air, which made her worry about the cost of getting it fixed. "I didn't have a lot of disposable income to replace a tire," said Howell.

She brought her car back to the shop that had done the accident repair, hoping the tire could be fixed as part of the insurance claim. But the mechanic refused to help her, insisting the tire had nothing to do with the accident. "It was frustrating," said Howell. "You're an auto repair shop. Couldn't you just take a look? It felt like all they cared about was dollars and cents."

That's when she remembered a previous positive experience with a tire shop called Discount Tire. Even though she hadn't purchased her tires there, she decided to give her local store a call.

"I called about 15 minutes before they closed, but they told me to bring it in and they'll take care of it." Howell was nervous about bringing her car in right before closing, but the friendly employee on the phone insisted.

A repair technician examined the tire when she got to the store and was able to patch it and reset the warning light in just a few minutes. The best part was there was no charge for the service!

"It was a relief," said Howell. "Why didn't I just go there first? After losing my job and getting in an accident, this was one less thing I had to worry about."

Tire problems can cause a lot of worry. Flat tires always seem to happen when you're running late to work, traveling far from home, or at some other inopportune time. Fixing them can take a bite out of your wallet, a bite out of your day, or both.

Discount Tire wins and retains customers by helping them recover from tire problems—even problems that aren't the company's fault. This includes offering free repairs on flat tires that can be safely patched. While you might expect this service as part of a good warranty on tires the company sells, it extends the service to customers like Howell who purchased their tires elsewhere.

This wasn't the first time Discount Tire had brought Howell some relief. A few years earlier, she'd gotten a flat tire shortly after purchasing her first new car. Howell had opted for the extended warranty, so she took her car to the dealership, thinking the warranty would cover the problem.

Unfortunately, the dealership didn't provide a Guaranteed Customer Experience. A service advisor pointed out the fine print in the warranty contract that excluded tires from coverage. Rather than find a way to help, the service advisor tried to take advantage of the situation and sell her a new tire.

To Howell, this didn't feel right. "I'm right out of college. I'm already paying my car payment. It felt like a lot of expenses."

She decided to get a second opinion before buying the tire. A friend suggested she go to Discount Tire, so she decided to give them a try. A technician brought the car into a service bay to examine the problem and returned a short while later with good news. The tire had been patched and the leak repaired! Best of all, there was no charge for the service.

In both situations, Howell was worried about the cost of fixing a tire. While other companies tried to profit from her misfortune, Discount Tire brought relief by quickly fixing the tire for free.

Helping customers recover from other companies' broken promises might seem like an expensive business strategy. Howell admitted she was surprised she didn't have to pay anything. But Discount Tire focuses on winning and retaining customers over the long run, not cashing in on the next sale. That's how the company earned a 4.1-star rating on Yelp across more than 1,000 stores in 35 states. Legions of loyal customers won't consider going anywhere else.[1]

"I love them!" said Leah Zachary, another loyal customer. "Discount Tire has been so customer service oriented about checking my tire pressure (for free) and repairing a slow leak (for free) that I don't even care how much their tires cost. When I need to buy tires, I just go there and say 'tell me what I need.' I buy from them because if they are taking that much time to hire and train their employees to such a high level of consistency in service, I know they've got the tire part figured out, too. I know I'm going to feel great when I leave there with my new tires. And since they take care of problems with tires they didn't even sell me, I feel confident they are going to stand behind what they sell."

There's a competitor located next door to my local Discount Tire shop. That company hung a large banner reading, "We beat Discount Tire's prices!" I'll never find out if it's true, because, like Howell and Zachary, Discount Tire has saved my day more than once by quickly repairing a flat tire at no charge.

The purchase experience has also been positive. The last time I needed to buy tires, the service advisor talked me into a less expensive model than the tires I asked for and assured me I would be much happier with them than if I selected the same model currently on my car. He was right—I was.

What Discount Tire fundamentally understands better than its competition is that winning customers and keeping them requires more than just focusing on the next sale. You have to make things right when a promise is broken. Customers are looking for relief, and nothing in the customer experience builds a stronger sense of relief than a fantastic service recovery.

How Great Recoveries Create Lasting Memories

There's a legendary story about a Nordstrom department store that allowed a customer to return a tire for a refund in 1975, even though the company doesn't sell tires. An elderly customer was apparently confused because Nordstrom had recently acquired the store from a company that did sell tires, so he went inside without realizing the change. Consultants, authors, and keynote speakers have used the story for years as an example of extraordinary customer service.

It's hard to tell if the story is true. The details vary depending on where the story is published, such as the amount of the refund and whether the customer returned one tire or two.[2] At least one newspaper article quotes unnamed Nordstrom officials as saying the story never happened.[3]

The story endures because it's a terrific example of making things right. It's rare for a company to offer refunds on tires, even if that's a product the company actually sells. Whatever was wrong with them, it clearly wasn't Nordstrom's fault.

In 1975, the same year the Nordstrom story allegedly occurred, Discount Tire ran its first television commercial. It depicted an elderly woman rolling a tire through a parking lot and then heaving it through the glass window of a Discount Tire store. "If ever you're not satisfied with one of our tires," said the narrator, "please feel free to bring it back."[4]

Discount Tire still accepts returned tires today. "If ever you're not satisfied with your purchase, bring it back and we will make it right," reads the return policy. "That is our promise. At Discount

Tire, we stand behind our products and services and want you to be completely satisfied with every item you purchase."[5]

Making it right is a critical component of the Guaranteed Customer Experience model. You can have the best product or service in the world, but problems happen, promises will be broken, and customers will be disappointed. It's essential that you have a recovery plan to handle these situations.

We briefly discussed the Peak-End Rule in Chapter 5, and it's worth a quick review here. Customers tend to remember the experience that's most unusual compared to the norm (the peak) and their last impression (the end). A service failure creates a strong negative peak that will also be the customer's end impression if there's no recovery. This memory can overshadow previous positive experiences and cause the customer to retain a negative overall impression of their experience.

On the other hand, a great recovery might be the single best opportunity to create a strong emotional bond with a customer. The recovery creates a new, positive peak, because it swings from the frustrating low of the service failure to the high of a successful resolution. It replaces the potential negative end of a service failure with a happy ending that cements the customer's positive memory.

I first discovered this concept many years ago when I ran a regular customer service training workshop for contact center agents at my company. The class began with a discussion of good and bad customer service, and participants were asked to share their own experiences as customers. Two themes emerged as I facilitated many sessions.

The first is that nearly every story about poor service focused on an employee who seemingly failed to do their job. There might have been a defective product or some other problem, but what really stood out was an employee's inability or unwillingness to make things right. The training participants were almost always more upset about the employee who didn't fix the issue than they were about the problem itself.

The second theme was that almost every story about good service also started with a service failure. A promise of some kind was broken, and the customer felt frustrated. The difference was that in the good stories, an employee stepped up and made things right. That service recovery created a lasting positive memory in the mind of the customer, overriding the disappointment of the initial problem.

Discount Tire succeeds because it offers its customers a great overall experience. It carries a wide selection of tires. It has knowledgeable and friendly employees who help customers get the right tires for their vehicles, even if the best tire choice is less expensive than other options. Service appointments are kept promptly, and walk-in customers can usually get fast service too.

The company really stands out when problems occur. If an employee sells a customer a set of tires and that customer is unhappy after driving on them, the customer will feel that a promise has been broken. It doesn't matter whether the tires were defective, the salesperson misrepresented the tires, or the customer did a poor job of explaining their needs. What matters is the recovery.

That's why Discount Tire promises to make things right. That could be a refund, exchanging the tires for a different model, or some other resolution that best fits the particular situation. There's no condition attached that stipulates the tires have to be defective, or that Discount Tire is even at fault.

In fact, Discount Tire wins a lot of customers by fixing problems a customer couldn't reasonably expect the company to take responsibility for solving. Neither of Chelsea Howell's flat tires were caused by Discount Tire. She hadn't even purchased the tires there. But Discount Tire still helped Howell recover by quickly fixing them for free.

Other companies also win and retain customers with strong recoveries. Zinus gives customers 100 nights to try any product, and customers can return their purchase for a full refund during that time. Zinus even pays for the return shipping. Osprey offers a lifetime warranty on its backpacks and will repair a pack no matter how old it is. Domino's offers Carryout Insurance, where it will replace a pizza at no cost if a customer accidentally damages it on the way home from picking it up.

Recall from Chapter 2 that Jenny Dempsey's plant initially struggled to grow after she bought it at an Armstrong Garden Center. It was only when she brought it back to the store that an employee recovered the experience by coaching Dempsey on how to restore the plant to health. The thriving plant is now Dempsey's peak experience with Armstrong—a strong, positive, lasting memory that has turned her into a loyal customer.

Problems will happen. Products break, services fall short, and employees make mistakes. Customers misuse products, have unreasonable expectations, and sometimes refuse to take responsibility even when they're the cause of the issue.

These situations are moments of truth for companies and individual employees. Recover well, and you form a positive, lasting memory that will likely earn you a loyal customer. Fail to recover, and the customer will probably harbor ill feelings for a long time to come.

What Happens When You Don't Recover from a Broken Promise

My dad is a car guy. He enjoys going to car shows, whether they feature classic cars or the latest models. He has an encyclopedic knowledge of cars and subscribes to several automotive magazines to keep up with the latest developments.

Buying a new car is a serious process for my dad. He starts thinking about options months in advance of a planned purchase. He conducts extensive research, test drives multiple cars, and negotiates happily with the most hard-nosed salespeople. My mom is always part of the process, especially when it comes to the financial decisions, but my dad is the one who really gets into it.

Car guys tend to be loyal to a specific brand. My dad is an Oldsmobile guy, a now-defunct brand once part of General Motors. He also likes Buick, another General Motors brand, and has owned several of each over the years.

When I was a kid, my dad decided to do something unimaginable for a guy who likes Oldsmobiles and Buicks. He bought a Ford.

It takes a lot for a loyal car enthusiast to switch brands, but this was a Ford Thunderbird. It had power, looks, and luxury. My dad already knew all that when he stepped onto the lot at the car dealership, but the salesperson was also very persuasive. He expertly showed off the car's features and helped my dad envision himself driving a car that an enthusiast would be proud to own.

The excitement of buying a new Thunderbird was short-lived. My dad was driving the car home when it died in the middle of the road. It completely shut down—the engine, the electronics, everything. Fortunately, he was in a quiet neighborhood when it happened, and he was able to safely push it out of the street.

This experience was the exact opposite of what the Ford salesperson had promised. There was no excitement, prestige, or performance. My dad certainly didn't feel cool pushing his new broken car out of the road!

The vehicle was towed back to the dealership, where the sales manager faced a moment of truth. Recovering from the extreme disappointment of a new car breaking down on its first drive was no easy task. That challenge got even more difficult when you consider my dad had been loyal to a competitor, and this was the first time he'd purchased a Ford.

My parents went to the dealership and requested a refund. At first, the sales manager flatly declined to take the car back and instead offered a lukewarm apology along with a promise to fix it. He attempted to dismiss the problem as a minor issue, without acknowledging the negative feelings that come with a new car breaking down on the ride home from the dealership. He was too worried about the financial impact to care about the terrible experience my parents were having.

You might recall from the Disneyland example in Chapter 7 that my mom is a master negotiator. She swatted away the sales manager's arguments like flies. My parents dug in their heels, and he finally relented and gave them a full refund. By then, the bad experiences and the sales manager's poor recovery had left a lasting negative impression. My dad, an Oldsmobile guy, never bought another Ford.

This auto dealership isn't alone in failing to recover from an epic letdown. Many companies make it difficult for customers to get relief after a service failure. Customer service teams are intentionally difficult to reach, with contact information buried on a website, lengthy interactions with automated service robots, and long waits to speak with someone in understaffed departments. Once a customer does get in contact with an actual human, employees frequently lack the authority to quickly fix obvious problems. Some problems get escalated to managers, who are so concerned about short-term losses that they stonewall any attempt at a meaningful remedy.

Leaders at these companies fail to understand the long-term impact of such short-sighted decisions. Unresolved service failures are emotional gut punches to a customer. They create a lasting negative memory of the experience that causes customers to re-evaluate whether to do business with a company.

Research conducted by marketing consultant and college administrator Venessa Funches revealed that customers frequently find ways to get back at companies that let them down. As you might expect, 42 percent stopped doing business with the company altogether, but Funches found other customers had ways to punish companies for unresolved service failures without leaving:

★ 35 percent bought less from the company

★ 25 percent stopped buying certain products or services

★ 17 percent stopped doing business with a particular location

Angry customers also make a concerted effort to tarnish the offending company's reputation. Funches found that 70 percent spread negative word-of-mouth via social media, online review sites, and by sharing stories with friends.[6]

An awkward recovery effort that fails to address the real issue can sometimes be just as damaging as no recovery at all. My wife, Sally, and I were having brunch at a restaurant, and Sally's meal wasn't prepared the way she expected. When our server came by our table and asked the perfunctory, "How's everything?" question, Sally gave honest feedback that she hoped would be passed along to the chef so the next guest might benefit.

Our server apologized, and then came back a short while later to offer us a free dessert. We thanked her, but politely declined. It was 11:00 am, and dessert wasn't very tempting.

The manager came to our table not long after that, apologized for Sally's disappointing meal, and again offered a free dessert. We again declined, but the manager was insistent. She told us she would have the dessert boxed up, so we could take it to go. Once again, we said no thank you.

When it came time to bring our check, sure enough, our server brought the dessert in a box and ceremoniously placed it on the table. Now we were annoyed, and a bit sad that the dessert would go to waste. While there's nothing inherently wrong with offering a free dessert when warranted, foisting something on a customer who repeatedly says "No" is aggressively poor service.

Ironically, our experience was okay until the free dessert debacle. Sally wasn't angry about her meal. She was mildly disappointed in the preparation and just wanted to share some honest feedback. It was the poor recovery attempt that turned our experience into a negative one and convinced us not to return to that restaurant.

Upset customers don't always want a discount or a free dessert. Many just want their complaints to be heard. Others would prefer to have the problem fixed rather than be offered compensation for accepting a poor experience.

Promises can and will get broken. Nothing is perfect. But the quality of your recovery effort will determine whether you create a fiercely loyal customer or an antagonistic ex-customer who makes it their mission to hurt your business.

Exercise: Describe What a Great Recovery Looks Like

Recovering from broken promises is the final piece of the Guaranteed Customer Experience model. To recap, the model has three elements:

1. Promise

2. Action

3. Recovery

In the next chapter, we'll get down to the nuts and bolts of creating a recovery process. For now, let's focus on the big picture. What should a great recovery look like?

You might want to download the workbook at guaranteedexperience.com/workbook and use the worksheet for Chapter 8 to help you with this exercise.

Start with the promise you created at the end of Chapter 4, and imagine that the promise was broken. It doesn't matter what caused it, whether it was a failure by your company, someone else's fault, or the customer merely perceived an issue.

Answer these two questions from the customer's perspective:

1. How does the customer feel about the broken promise?

2. What would make the customer feel great again?

There are several ways to get answers to these questions. One is through direct customer feedback. You'll likely already have clear and specific feedback from upset customers, along with (hopefully) examples of customers who experienced a fantastic recovery.

A recovery process becomes more relevant when we can empathize with our customers' feelings. This is sometimes easy to do—if you see someone bump their head on a cabinet, you instinctively cringe because you know exactly how that feels. At other times, empathy is more difficult if you've never experienced the same issue or you're too wrapped up in your own problems.

I worked in a clothing store when I was a teenager. My least favorite activity was processing customer returns. It was a very manual process back then that took a long time to complete and would often draw impatient looks from waiting customers. Early on, I struggled with returns because I was focused on the problems they caused me, rather than the problems my customer was experiencing.

Over time, with a lot of practice and coaching from my manager, I learned to focus on my customer. This actually took the pressure off of me, and I felt better about what I was doing when I concentrated on helping them. My display of genuine concern and my upbeat, positive attitude had a calming effect on the other customers in line, who were more patient when they saw me cheerfully helping a customer with a return.

Here's an exercise that can help you tap into empathy for your customer. Start by imagining once again that your promise has been broken.

1. How does your customer feel?

2. Why do they feel that way?

3. Have you ever had a similar feeling?

The similar feeling doesn't have to come from an identical issue. It can come from a completely different scenario that made you feel the same way.

For example, a technical support employee might field a call from a customer having trouble setting up the company's app on their smartphone. The technical support rep might struggle to empathize with the customer at first, since they themselves are highly proficient with the app and couldn't imagine experiencing the same problem. However, these empathy questions can help the employee understand the customer's feelings.

The first question is, "How does your customer feel?" They might recognize that the customer is frustrated because they can't get the app to work.

The next question is, "Why does the customer feel that way?" The employee might understand that the customer feels helpless and a little dumb because they can't figure it out themselves, and annoyed that they're spending time trying to fix the problem rather than doing something else on their to-do list.

The third question is, "Have you ever had a similar feeling?" The support rep might think of a time when they felt helpless about a problem, such as a recent experience with a leaking toilet that required a plumber to repair it. The feeling of helplessness because they couldn't fix the toilet themselves, the annoyance of taking time off work for the plumber's visit, and the anxiety about receiving a hefty bill could all be unpleasant memories that help the rep understand how their customer is feeling about the smartphone app.

Once you have an empathetic understanding of how your customers feel when a promise is broken, you can think of ways to help your customer feel great again. For instance, the tech support rep might realize from their experience with a plumber that what their customers want more than anything is reassurance that the support rep will help them quickly fix the issue without making them feel stupid.

After you create a clear picture of what a great recovery looks like, we can move on to Chapter 9, where we'll create a plan to make it happen.

Chapter 8 Notes

1   Discount Tire's overall Yelp rating is based on aggregate review data provided by Yelp.

2   There's an excellent overview of the Nordstrom tire legend written by David Mikkelson on the Snopes website, accessed August 26, 2020, https://www.snopes.com/fact-check/return-to-spender/.

3   Lena H. Sun, "Many Happy Returns," *Washington Post*, December 26, 1988.

4   You can watch the commercial on Discount Tire's YouTube channel, accessed August 26, 2020 https://youtu.be/TE1dFHmFCRk.

5   Discount Tire return policy, posted on the Discount Tire website, accessed August 26, 2020, https://www.discounttire.com/customer-service/return-policy.

6   Venessa Funches, "The consumer anger phenomena: causes and consequences," *Journal of Services Marketing*, September 13, 2001.

Chapter 9
HOW TO CREATE A RECOVERY PLAN

There are two truths about luggage for frequent travelers.

The first truth is that your luggage will get damaged. It's only a matter of time for even the best-made items. Bags get tossed, slammed, grabbed, pinched, and pulled. I once lost a zipper pull on my computer bag when it got stuck underneath the airline seat in front of me. The pull snapped clean off as I extricated my bag.

The second truth about luggage is that repairs cause anxiety. Road warriors have a routine. They have a special way of packing that they do unconsciously because they do it so often. It causes real disruption if the routine is broken by taking a favorite suitcase out of the lineup for even one trip.

My wife, Sally, was a road warrior for many years. She regularly flew more than 100,000 miles annually in her job managing process improvement projects for a hotel chain. Her suitcase was dragged through airports, stowed on airplanes, dumped into taxis, and stashed in hotel rooms nearly every week.

After the first few years of extensive travel, Sally noticed her bags weren't up to the grind. For example, her computer bag would wear out every year and need replacing. She decided to invest in a bag that would withstand the rigors of extensive travel.

At the time, Tumi was probably the most well-known brand for corporate travelers. Its bags were expensive but marketed as tough enough to last for years. Tumi was also known for having a good warranty and had a reputation as a company that stood behind its products. So Sally went to her local Tumi store and picked out a Tumi computer bag.

It was a trial run of sorts. Her rollaboard suitcase was also wearing out and would soon need replacing. If the computer bag worked well, Sally planned to invest in a Tumi suitcase.

But the new computer bag was a bust. The zipper broke after just six weeks of use. The Tumi bag didn't even last as long as the less-expensive bags it replaced!

Sally was disappointed in the bag's poor quality, but assumed the zipper could easily be fixed under the bag's warranty. She took it back to the Tumi shop, where the bad news got worse. The only way to get the bag repaired was to send it to a repair center in another state. The employee estimated Sally would be without her bag for at least six weeks.

This isn't helpful for a road warrior who uses her bag nearly every week. Sally inquired about a faster option, such as a local repair service, but was told the bag had to be shipped to the out-of-state repair depot. She asked about a loaner bag to get her through her next few trips, but was informed that the company didn't provide loaners.

Tumi, the company with the reputation for making indestructible bags for frequent travelers, let Sally down. It broke its promise to solve her problem of needing a tough bag for travel. And when the bag broke, Tumi failed to make it right.

Sally returned the Tumi bag for a refund and bought a new bag from Coach. Several years later, it still looks great and hasn't let her down. Meanwhile, she still needed a new rollaboard suitcase that could hold up to her extensive travel schedule. Tumi was obviously no longer in the running.

I accompanied her to John's Fifth Avenue Luggage in San Diego. (The family-owned store is now called Index Urban, and they're still great.) A helpful employee greeted us, and Sally explained what she needed. With no hesitation, the employee pointed us to a display of Briggs & Riley suitcases and recommended them as the best option for frequent travelers. Sally picked out a new rollaboard suitcase that met her needs.

The bag was amazing. It was clearly designed by people who understood travelers and was loaded with innovative features. The outer shell of the bag was ballistic nylon, which is an incredibly durable fabric that resists scratches, scuffs, and tears. Inside was a unique compression system that expanded the bag for packing and then compressed everything to fit in a smaller space. The telescoping handle was fixed outside the bag, rather than inside like most rollaboards, which left more room for clothes and created a flat space at the bottom.

The best thing about the bag might have been the Briggs & Riley Simple As That® guarantee. Briggs & Riley promised to repair the bag if it was ever damaged, even if the damage was caused by an airline. Even better, John's Fifth Avenue Luggage was an authorized repair center, which meant any repairs could quickly be done on-site. This was a major selling point, given Sally's experience that all bags eventually needed some sort of repair.

Sally's rollaboard worked great on the road. She loved hers so much that I bought the same Briggs & Riley suitcase several months later when it came time to replace my own rollaboard. It was tough, dependable, and easy to pack. That was nearly ten years ago, and both of our suitcases still look and work great.

A few years after she bought it, a zipper pull broke. It was the kind of normal wear that happens from the abuse of constant travel, but Sally was nervous about the repair process. Would Briggs & Riley really honor its warranty after several years?

She took the bag to John's Fifth Avenue Luggage and was promised an easy fix at no charge. The repair took just three days, so she was able to get the bag fixed between trips. When Sally picked up her bag, the employee pointed out that the repair technician had noticed that a couple of the suitcase's handles were starting to wear, so those had been replaced as well.

Experiences like this have made Sally and me loyal Briggs & Riley customers. We recommend the bags to friends, and it's the only brand we'll consider when it's time to purchase a new bag. I recently replaced my computer bag with a Briggs & Riley backpack that's remarkably well-designed and functional. While my last computer bag lasted through an impressive seven years of travel and frequent abuse, I expect my new Briggs & Riley backpack to last even longer.

The bags themselves are terrific, but it's the recovery process that really cemented our loyalty. Unlike the competitor, whose plan would have left Sally without a bag for six weeks, Briggs & Riley has a repair process that makes it easy for customers to get their bags fixed and keep on traveling.

The Elements of a Great Recovery Plan

It's inevitable that promises will sometimes be broken. That's why companies offering a Guaranteed Customer Experience have a recovery plan in place, so they can act swiftly to fix problems and restore the customer's faith in the company, its products, and its services.

As Sally learned from her luggage repair experiences, promising a customer you'll take care of a problem and then actually doing what you promised are two different things. This is where Briggs & Riley shines. Its repair process showcases the three elements of a great recovery plan:

1. Solve the problem
2. Make it easy
3. Restore faith

Element #1: Solve the customer's problem

Throughout this book, we've focused on the importance of understanding the customer's true problem. Solving that problem needs to be the focus of a good recovery process.

A broken zipper isn't the real issue for a frequent traveler like Sally. Nor is getting it fixed at no charge under warranty. Neither of those matter if the process leaves the traveler without a bag to use for weeks at a time. The true problem is needing a reliable bag for the next trip.

The Briggs & Riley repair process is designed to give customers multiple options for expediting repairs. One is to take the bag to a local repair center, like Sally did when a zipper pull broke on her rollaboard. The repair only took a few days, but a loaner bag would have been available if Sally's suitcase had needed more extensive and lengthy repairs.

Another option is to send the bag to a Briggs & Riley repair center. Here again, the company is sensitive to its customers' travel needs. One reviewer commented that when he needed his briefcase for a business trip in two weeks, the Briggs & Riley repair center was able to expedite the repair and ship it back in less than one week.

Briggs & Riley also provides self-repair kits that can be shipped to customers for simpler fixes. This gives customers the option to quickly fix a handle, wheel, or other bag part on their own without waiting for a repair center to process a warranty claim and return the suitcase.

Other companies you've met throughout this book take a similar approach to fixing the customer's true problem when things go wrong. Similar to Briggs & Riley, Osprey allows customers to ship their backpack to Osprey for a repair, or it will send parts, so customers can make simple repairs themselves and quickly get back on the trail. TriMet monitors its system so it can send a replacement bus or reroute passengers in the event of significant delays, so people can get to their destination on time. Discount Tire patches flat tires at no charge, so car owners can get their vehicle back on the road quickly.

In many ways, a recovery plan is like its own experience guarantee. It starts by understanding the customer's true problem, making a promise to fix it, and then taking action to keep that promise.

Customer service employees make a huge impact on customer experience when they become adept at identifying a customer's true problem. However, this can be difficult when situations happen quickly or there's no clear policy to follow. Sometimes employees need to rely on their own instincts to find a fast solution.

For example, a mom and her two young kids went out to the movies and stopped at the concession stand to load up on popcorn and soda before heading into the theater. Just as they left the counter, one of the kids spilled his drink on the floor. Suddenly, the mom had several problems that all caused anxiety. She worried about:

★ Having to clean up the spill.

★ Her child getting upset.

★ Having to wait in line to buy a new soda.

★ The extra cost of a replacement drink.

★ Missing the start of the movie.

What do you think was her true problem?

The real issue was the mom wanted to enjoy a movie with her kids. The soda spill and the resulting worries threatened to make the experience a lot less pleasant.

Fortunately, the quick-thinking cashier recognized the customer's true problem when he saw her child spill the soda and the resulting worried expression on her face. He politely paused his interaction with the next customer in line and offered the mom a replacement drink at no charge. The cashier then assured her he would have the spill cleaned up, so she and her kids could go enjoy the movie. He called another coworker over and asked for help with the spill so nobody would accidentally slip, and he then went back to the customer he'd been serving.

The relief was evident on the mom's face as she and her kids resumed their trip into the theater. The solution took less than a minute and cost the theater less than a dollar to solve, but it added a positive peak to the mom's experience.

Element #2: Make it easy

Companies following the Guaranteed Customer Experience model strive to remove friction from the recovery process wherever they can. The goal is to make the recovery as easy as possible.

Making a recovery process easy often starts with product development. According to Richard Krulik, Briggs & Riley's CEO, the company includes the repair department when designing new suitcases. The ultimate goal is to create durable bags that don't need to be repaired. Recognizing that some damage is inevitable, the bags are also designed with the repair process in mind. The easier a suitcase is to repair, the sooner a customer can take the bag on their next trip.

"Our design team collaborates intricately with our repair team during the design process to assess for any areas that need changing or improving. Part of that effort ensures that the way the bags are designed will allow for easy repairs. A simple example would be the placement of a seam to make a repair easier."

Small design changes can make a big impact. For instance, Briggs & Riley uses screws rather than rivets to assemble many of its bag components. Krulik explains how this choice was made to give customers more options for fixing a damaged bag. "While screws cost a lot more as well as take longer in manufacturing, they allow for easier repairs by the consumer, who we can send a part to so they are not without the bag for several weeks."

Other elements of the repair process are designed to be as frictionless as possible. Customers can order replacement parts online if they wish to repair their bag themselves. If they want to send the bag to Briggs & Riley, they only need to complete a short return authorization form and then ship the bag. The Briggs & Riley website also has a list of authorized repair centers, so customers can find a local repair shop to get the job done.

When Sally brought her rollaboard back to John's Fifth Avenue Luggage to get a zipper pull repaired, she didn't have to gather the receipt or warranty registration card. The warranty covered the repair regardless of who owned the bag, where it was purchased, or how long Sally had owned it. The only paperwork involved was a short claim form the employee filled out that identified the bag as Sally's, described the repair to be made, and indicated the date when it would be ready for pickup. The entire drop-off process took less than five minutes.

Organizations that offer a Guaranteed Customer Experience ensure that employees are empowered to quickly recover from broken promises. I researched empowerment best practices while writing *The Service Culture Handbook* and was surprised to discover that empowerment is more than just giving people more authority. Customer-focused companies define empowerment as *enabling* employees to provide a great experience—and to recover when something goes wrong.

Employees need three things to empower them to recover quickly from broken promises and service failures:

1. Resources

2. Procedures

3. Authority

Resources include the supplies, materials, and tools necessary to get the job done. Briggs & Riley stocks replacement parts it can send to customers who want to repair bags themselves. It's created an online ordering system that makes it easy for bag owners to identify the part they need and request it. This system not only makes things easier for customers, it allows Briggs & Riley to keep track of parts inventory and requests for self-repair kits. (You'd be surprised at how many companies lack a system for managing spare parts.)

Procedures represent a consistent way of doing things. The bag repair procedures are clearly outlined on the Briggs & Riley website, giving customers confidence that the process will be handled effectively. It also gives customer service employees a clear roadmap to follow when assisting customers, so customers have a consistent experience.

Authority allows employees to exercise discretion without first seeking approval. At Briggs & Riley, this even extends to third-party repair centers. Recall that the handles on Sally's bag were replaced without even asking, because the repair technician noticed they were getting worn and would soon need to be replaced anyway. There was no paperwork, no approval process, and no delay. The employee had the authority to just make it happen, because it was the right thing to do.

Other customer-focused companies succeed by making the recovery process as easy as possible.

Amazon makes it extremely easy to return most purchases. Customers go to the website, indicate the item they want to return, and receive a return slip that can be stored digitally on a phone or printed out. The item can be dropped off at any authorized location, such as a UPS store, where an employee scans the return slip to record it in the computer and then takes the item. Customers don't even need to box it up for shipping—the employee handles all that and ships it back to Amazon on the customer's behalf. Best of all, the return is immediately credited to the customer's account as soon as the return slip is scanned.

GreatAmerica strives to have a live person answer customer calls within two rings. Calls don't get routed through an automated system or go to voice mail. Phone menus, waiting on hold, and leaving voice messages all create friction for a customer trying to solve a problem.

Discount Tires keeps room in its schedule for walk-in customers. This has helped me on multiple occasions when I've gotten a nail in a tire and needed a repair right away. Even on a busy morning,

I've typically gotten in and out in less than an hour with minimal disruption to my day.

The easier you make the recovery process for your customers, the faster you can move them from *disappointment* over a broken promise to *relief* that the problem has been solved.

Element #3: Restore faith

The recovery process is an opportunity to restore a customer's faith in your brand, product, or even an individual employee. When done properly, a great recovery can signal to customers that problems are infrequent and any issues will be quickly and thoroughly handled. It becomes a positive memory instead of a lingering negative one.

Krulik told me that Briggs & Riley's industry-leading warranty was originally created to give customers confidence that the unusual placement of the handle would actually work. "The telescoping handle being on the back of the case made so much sense, similar to how a dresser drawer has the rails underneath rather than inside the drawer. The Simple As That® warranty was created at first to assure consumers that our handle would withstand the rigors of baggage handlers."

That assurance would ring hollow if broken handles were a regular occurrence or the company didn't have a great procedure to facilitate any necessary repairs. Fortunately, the suitcases are both well-designed and durable. Neither Sally nor I have had issues with the handles on our Briggs & Riley rollaboards over the years we've owned them. It's comforting to know that the repair process is easy to navigate should something break in the future.

Briggs & Riley also restores faith in its products by fixing damage caused by airlines. The damage claim process for many airlines is a frustrating maze of paperwork, delays, and obfuscation. It can take more than a month to get compensated, and getting updated information can be difficult. Briggs & Riley owners avoid all that, simply by getting their bag repaired under warranty without involving the airline.

This is all part of the company's strategy to win and retain customers. According to Krulik, "The Simple As That warranty has since become part of our overall vision, which is 'To build lifelong customers that advocate passionately and proudly for our brand.' In that regard, we do much more than just the warranty. Our everyday pricing, intelligent and innovative designs, unmatched durability, and great customer service all have the brand vision as the filter in our decisions and actions. We want Briggs & Riley to be the brand that consumers will always come to for their luggage and brag to all their friends and family about."

Sometimes restoring faith requires a company or individual to demonstrate that they're working hard on the customer's behalf. When GreatAmerica's headquarters in Cedar Rapids, Iowa, flooded in 2008, the company quickly implemented an emergency response plan. Employees relocated to backup facilities, home offices, coffee shops, and hotels and continued to serve customers. Damage from the flood kept employees out of the headquarters building for two months, but the company remained focused on taking care of customers the entire time. Whatever worries customers might have had about the flood interrupting the service they expected from GreatAmerica were quickly assuaged when the company didn't miss a beat.

Briggs & Riley, GreatAmerica, Discount Tire, and other companies offering a Guaranteed Customer Experience all have clear recovery plans. They go to great lengths to restore customers' faith when things go wrong and are rewarded with lasting customer loyalty and advocacy.

What Happens if You Don't Have a Recovery Plan

Ben "Lucky" Schlappig writes for the popular travel blog *One Mile at a Time*. He shares tips for maximizing airline, hotel, and credit card loyalty programs. As someone who travels approximately 400,000 miles per year, he puts a lot of wear and tear on his suitcase.

Schlappig used his blog to chronicle a frustrating repair experience with Tumi that mirrored Sally's. His suitcase had a few missing zipper pulls and a squeaky wheel that he wanted replaced, so he took the bag to his local Tumi store. There, an employee informed him that the suitcase could be fixed for a $26 processing fee and would be shipped to a Tumi repair facility. The employee assured Schlappig that the $26 fee was all that was required, and the bag would be fixed under warranty at no additional charge.

He received an email from Tumi several days later with disappointing news. It informed him that the repair would not be covered under warranty as originally promised, and it would cost an additional $177 to fix the bag and ship it back to him.

Schlappig wrote back and complained about the disparity between what the store employee told him and what the repair center was now saying. Rather than honor the store employee's promise, the customer service employee offered him a discount on a new bag.

Fortunately, Schlappig had just purchased a Briggs & Riley suitcase to replace the Tumi, so the repair process wouldn't leave him without a suitcase to travel with. He'd planned to get the Tumi bag fixed and then give it to his dad, but he didn't feel the old suitcase was worth the cost. So he wrote back to Tumi's customer service department and asked them to donate his old bag instead of charging him more to return it.[1]

The experienced cemented Schlappig's decision to become a Briggs & Riley customer. What should have been an easy repair on the Tumi bag became a string of broken promises that alienated him from the brand after being a loyal customer for many years. Documenting his experiences on his blog also sent a clear signal to thousands of potential customers that Briggs & Riley offered a superior customer experience.

Companies that lack a recovery plan fail to solve the problem, don't make it easy for customers to get help, and certainly don't restore faith in the company's ability to keep its promises. The recovery process, not the initial problem, is often what convinces upset customers to take their business to the competition.

Schlappig expected his bag would eventually wear out. They all do, especially after traveling for hundreds of thousands of miles. What he did not expect was getting a runaround when he tried to get his bag repaired.

Many customer service employees would love to solve the problems their customers face, but they lack the resources, procedures, and authority to do so. I was once issued a gift card instead of a refund for an online purchase I had returned. The item was defective, and a cash refund was within the company's return policy, but an error in the return process caused the gift card to be issued instead.

I contacted customer service, and the polite rep acknowledged the problem but told me there was nothing he could do to fix it. His computer system wouldn't allow it. My call was escalated to a supervisor who told me the same thing—he saw the obvious error, but he lacked the ability to fix it. The supervisor finally agreed to do some additional research and follow up via email with a resolution. But I never got that email.

Customers find it hard to trust a company when it won't fix obvious errors. These experiences tend to have a compounding effect that exacerbates the initial problem. In my case, what started as one service failure ultimately became four:

★ The purchased item was defective (service failure #1).

★ A gift card was issued instead of a refund (service failure #2).

★ The customer service department couldn't fix the refund error (service failure #3).

★ The supervisor didn't follow up (service failure #4).

I probably would have remained a loyal customer if the company had promptly and accurately recovered from the initial disappointment of a defective purchase. Instead, the lack of a recovery plan made the situation worse by wasting my time and money, and I went to a competitor the next time I needed something similar.

It's my experience that executives fail to create adequate recovery plans because of a series of false assumptions. They assume:

★ Promises won't be broken.

★ The cost of recovery will outweigh the benefit.

★ Employees can't be trusted to use their discretion.

There's a simple way to test those assumptions. Monitor your customer experience to detect and track broken promises (see Chapter 7), calculate your "customer math" to understand the financial impact (see Chapter 5), and experiment with trusting your employees to do the right thing for customers.

It's that last one, mistrusting employees, that's usually the biggest false choice. You don't need to give employees wide latitude to do whatever they want to make a customer happy. You just need to give them the ability to do the right thing.

Exercise: Create a Recovery Plan

Goodwill discounts, apologies, and other gestures of atonement are all fine, but none of those matter if your recovery process doesn't solve the customer's problem.

This exercise will walk you through the steps to create a recovery plan. There's a worksheet in the downloadable exercise workbook at guaranteedexperience.com/workbook to help you out.

Start building your recovery process by reconnecting with your customer's "I need to _____" statement. Remind yourself of the original problem they're trying to solve and the promise you made to solve it.

1. Now use these three questions to craft a plan to make things right if something goes wrong:

2. How can you solve the customer's problem?

3. How can you make the solution as easy as possible for your customer?

How can you restore your customer's faith in you?

No plan can anticipate every circumstance. Employees might occasionally encounter a broken promise they aren't equipped to solve. A good recovery plan should include a way for employees to use their best judgement or escalate those unusual or difficult issues to someone who can fix them.

Chapter 9 Notes

1   Ben Schlappig, "Tumi's Disappointing Customer Service," *One Mile at a Time* blog, June 28, 2019.

Chapter 10
END HERE

Joe Namath's Super Bowl III guarantee might be the most famous guarantee in sports.

The 1969 contest featured the Baltimore Colts versus the New York Jets. Few expected the Jets to prevail over the heavily-favored Colts in the game played in Miami, Florida. By kickoff, odds-makers had the Colts winning by 18 points.

Namath, the Jets' quarterback, attended a banquet at the Miami Touchdown Club three days before the game. He was there to be recognized as the "Outstanding Professional Football Player of 1968."

Namath's acceptance speech started with the usual remarks, thanking his parents, coaches, and teammates. And then he said something shocking: "We are going to win on Sunday. I guarantee it!"

The next day, the *Miami Herald* published a headline in its sports section reading, "Namath Guarantees Jet Victory." His teammates were initially surprised and upset. Guaranteeing a victory was seen as taunting the other team and giving them extra motivation—something you just didn't do. Other players had made a point to be complimentary of the Colts in their media interviews, and now Namath was stirring up trouble. The Jets coach, Weeb Ewbank, was seen admonishing Namath the next morning at breakfast in the team's hotel.

That initial reaction to Namath's guarantee gave way to a renewed sense of confidence. The team really did think they were better than the Colts and were resentful of the relentless press coverage painting the Jets as the underdog with no chance of winning. Days earlier, Ewbank himself had made similar remarks to his assistant coaches. "We can beat these guys. We're going to win this game."[1]

The Jets pulled off a stunning victory, winning 16-7. Namath played well enough to earn the Super Bowl MVP award, and the Jets defense held the Colts scoreless until late in the fourth quarter. It's considered one of the greatest upsets in Super Bowl history.

The win gave Namath's guarantee legendary status, and it's still talked about more than 50 years later. There's just one problem with the story that gets very little coverage.

What Namath said wasn't a guarantee.

A guarantee contains three components. The first is a promise. The second is action to fulfill the promise. And the third is a recovery plan to make things right if the promise isn't kept.

Namath and his Jets won the game, but what if they hadn't? There was no remedy attached to Namath's promise. He was never prepared to make things right if he broke his promise and the Jets lost.

History is filled with sports figures who made similar promises of victory, only to see those promises broken when their team lost. Those statements are revealed as empty hype when those same people avoid accountability.

University of Wyoming football coach, Joe Glenn, guaranteed victory over rival Utah in 2007, only to see his team lose the game 50-0. Glenn offered nothing but a meek apology after the game. "I'd probably like to have it back now," he said. "I wouldn't do it again. Find the crow, and I'll eat it."[2]

Dan Gilbert, owner of the Cleveland Cavaliers NBA franchise, promised a championship after the Cavaliers' star player, LeBron James, left the team for rival Miami Heat in 2010. Gilbert wrote an open letter to fans, stating, "I personally guarantee that the

Cleveland Cavaliers will win an NBA Championship before the self-titled former 'king' wins one."[3]

Gilbert didn't keep his promise. No remedy was offered to Cavaliers fans when James and the Heat won the championship two years later, in 2012. Meanwhile, the Cavaliers suffered through two losing seasons and failed to make the playoffs during those same years. The team had to wait until 2016 to win their first-ever championship, after James returned to the Cavaliers as a free agent.

Namath's guarantee isn't even the only Super Bowl guarantee made by someone in the Jets organization. In 2011, the Jets head coach, Rex Ryan, guaranteed the Jets would win the Super Bowl in the upcoming season.[4] The team finished with an 8-8 record and failed to make the playoffs. Ryan did nothing to make amends for the letdown other than promising to stop making guarantees.[5]

A promise must be backed by action to make it a guarantee. This includes taking specific steps to keep the promise and having a way to make things right if it's broken. Otherwise, the promise is just puffery.

It's easy to make empty promises to customers. A dry cleaner helps a customer feel better when they promise to clean a suit in time for a special event, but causes a service failure when they forget to mention the store will be closed on the day the customer intends to pick it up. An electrician promising a same-day service call brings momentary relief, but ultimately creates disappointment when they never show up and don't return messages. An insurance agent who promises to "be there" for a client creates a sense of confidence, until the agent fails to return the client's call when the client needs to file a claim.

Customers are tired of being fooled. A company promising 99 percent uptime sounds impressive, until you do the math and realize that works out to more than seven hours of *downtime* per month. Marketing messages are filled with terms like *best in class, premier, leading, world class,* and other phrases that are completely empty unless they're backed up with real action. Warranties promising to make things right are useless if they're so full of fine print that customers can't easily hold companies to their word.

This is perhaps the most important lesson about implementing a Guaranteed Customer Experience. Saying "I guarantee it" does not make something a guarantee. Whether it's sports or business, if you make a promise, you have to be prepared to back it up.

Real Guarantees Require Commitment

Courtney Paris is an example of an athlete who made a real guarantee. Paris played basketball for the University of Oklahoma from 2005 to 2009, where she was a stand-out center and set multiple records. As her senior season drew to a close, Paris gave a speech at Oklahoma's senior night, promising that the team would win the upcoming NCAA women's basketball championship.

Paris pledged to repay her scholarship, worth $64,000, if she couldn't keep her promise.[6] "It might take me the rest of my life, but I will pay back my scholarship because I didn't do what I said I would do."[7]

Oklahoma started strong and advanced all the way to the Final Four in the tournament. The team fell short of its ultimate goal when it lost to Louisville 61-59 in the semifinals. The loss put Paris's words to the test.

She was asked about the guarantee after the game. "I do make good on the guarantee," said Paris. "Not today, though. Obviously, I don't have $64,000 waiting, but I do make good on it."[8]

The next day, Oklahoma athletic director Joe Castiglione announced that the university had no intention of collecting Paris's scholarship money. "It's even more meaningful when someone who committed herself for four years to help her teammates become better, making that kind of symbolic gesture," Castiglione said. "But having said that, I don't know of anyone who has had any expectation whatsoever that we would accept the monetary aspect of that gesture."[9]

Since Oklahoma wouldn't let Paris repay her scholarship, she decided to work with the university to set up a fund to benefit the local community. "We have a great, great university, and our athletic director wouldn't accept the money back," Paris said. "But I feel like there is something I can do to help the state of Oklahoma because they've supported me so much and I've had the best four years playing with them."[10]

A real guarantee requires this type of commitment. It's not enough to tell someone, "I guarantee it." The promise has to be backed by actions.

My wife, Sally, and I replaced the roof on our home after the old roof started to show signs of wear. One of the selling points was a 10-year warranty. This gave us confidence that we would be covered if something went wrong.

A few years later, the roof began leaking during an unusually heavy storm. It was still well within the warranty period, so I called the roofing company. The company was busy because the storm had triggered quite a few service calls, but a technician finally came out to the house several days later. He inspected the area and told me the leak wasn't coming from the roof, but from a gap where the eaves met the chimney. In other words, the leak wasn't covered by the warranty.

We had our house painted a short time later, and I mentioned the leak to the painting crew. They assured me they would pay special attention to the chimney area and seal any gaps they saw. Fortunately, we didn't have any heavy rains for the rest of the season, and the leak didn't return that year.

But it did reappear when heavy rains came back a year later. I crawled up into the attic to staunch the flow of water and investigate the source, but couldn't determine exactly where the water was getting in. This presented me with a dilemma. Was the painter responsible for not sealing the leak, or did the roofer mislead me about the true source of the problem? Could it be something else?

I contacted the roofer the next day, but never heard back. Then I called the painter and spoke to John Peek, the owner of Peek

Brothers Painting. Peek and his crew have done many paint jobs at our home over the years, and they always stand by their work. Peek agreed to come out later that day and inspect the issue.

Peek came to the house as promised and climbed up a ladder on the side of the house near the chimney. He told me he saw a hole in the roof flashing next to the chimney where the water appeared to be getting in, making it almost certain that the roof was the problem.

While he was up on the ladder, Peek noticed a few spots in the eaves that needed some touch-up paint. It was near the end of the day, so he asked if he could leave his ladder and come back the next day to do the touch-up. I was disappointed in the roofer, but grateful that Peek was willing to stand by his company's work and help me as much as he could.

Thirty minutes after he left, I heard a noise on the side of the house that sounded like someone climbing a ladder. I walked around and saw Don Teemsma, the owner of Ideal Plumbing, Heating, Air, and Electrical. Teemsma's company is another organization we know and trust that's done a lot of work at our home, but I was surprised to see him scaling John Peek's ladder on the side of our house!

Teemsma explained that Peek had given him a call and alerted him to another potential source of the leak. The refrigerant lines from our air conditioning system ran from the condenser unit outside, up to the attic where the rest of the system is located. The lines entered the attic near the leak, and Peek had noticed the lines didn't appear to be fully sealed. He alerted Teemsma, and Teemsma tried to contact me to see if he could come take a look. I missed his call, but since he was in the neighborhood, he came out to the house anyway and used Peek's ladder to inspect the problem.

In the end, it wasn't the paint job or the refrigerant lines. The roof flashing around the chimney hadn't been properly installed, and a hole developed in the flashing that let water in when we had particularly heavy rain.

The roofing company had broken its promise by doing a faulty installation. The technician broke the promise a second time by denying that the problem was their responsibility. The company had gone out of business by the time the leak reappeared, so the warranty was now useless. I had to pay another roofing company to fix the problem.

John Peek and Don Teemsma continued to earn our trust because they demonstrated their willingness to go the extra mile to keep their promises and make things right. They cared about taking responsibility, even after it became clear their companies didn't cause the problem. As a result, we've continued to hire Peek Brothers Painting and Ideal Plumbing, Heating, Air, and Electrical at every opportunity, and we never hesitate to recommend them to friends and neighbors. Since I'm writing about them in this book, you might even say I'm a customer evangelist.

Implementing a Guaranteed Customer Experience takes commitment. The type of commitment Courtney Paris made when she promised to repay her scholarship if her team didn't win and then still found a way to make it right when the University of Oklahoma let her off the hook. The type of commitment that John Peek and Don Teemsma show to their respective customers that's helped them earn repeat business year after year. The commitment you've seen from many of the companies you've met in this book—companies that go to great lengths to keep their promises.

Take Action

If you've gotten this far but haven't yet completed the exercises at the end of each chapter, I recommend you go back and do them now.

The exercises are designed to walk you through the process of creating a Guaranteed Customer Experience for your brand, for a specific product or service, or for the individual customers you serve. You'll find a workbook to help you at guaranteedexperience.com/workbook.

My friend, Sarah, is a baker, and she's taught me the importance of following a recipe precisely. Even the smallest change can alter the results. For example, I've discovered that one of Sarah's secrets to making her famous peanut-butter cookies taste so amazing is letting the butter warm up to room temperature before she mixes it into the cookie dough. The cookies really do taste more buttery if the butter starts out at room temperature instead of adding it right out of the refrigerator when it's chilled.

So be careful to complete each exercise thoroughly before moving to the next step. You might not get the results you want if you skip parts of the model or pick and choose what you want to implement.

There are a number of ways to get support if you get stuck at any point. One option is to contact me directly:

★ **Call or text**: 619-955-7946

★ **Email**: jeff@toistersolutions.com

Another option is to subscribe to my Inside Customer Service blog, where I post analyses, tips, and trends that can help you win and retain more customers. You'll find the blog at toistersolutions.com/blog.

This book's guarantee becomes effective once you complete the exercises and implement the Guaranteed Customer Experience model:

> *You will gain something from reading this book that you can use to win and retain more customers. I will give you a free one-hour phone coaching session if you implement the Guaranteed Customer Experience model and are not happy with the results.*

Using the guarantee is easy. If you're unhappy with the results you achieved from implementing the Guaranteed Customer Experience model, simply use this link to schedule a one-hour call with me at a date and time of your choosing: guaranteedexperience.com/guarantee.

Some people have asked me why I put my personal contact information in every book I write, or why I'm offering a guarantee to you for reading this book. The answer is simple: I'm trying to model the same concepts I'm sharing with you. What I want more than anything is to help you succeed, and making it easy to contact me is part of my commitment to your success. I'm so committed to this concept that I'm willing to offer a guarantee to back it up.

Now it's your turn to assess your own commitment. Are you willing to put in the work to:

★ Understand the problem your customer is trying to solve?

★ Make a compelling promise to fix that problem?

★ Do what it takes to keep your word?

★ Make things right if that promise is ever broken?

The companies and individuals who make these commitments are few and far between. Not everyone will be up for the challenge. If they were, then every gas station and convenience store would have a clean and fully operational restroom. But they don't.

I called this chapter "End Here" because it's the end of the book. Now it's your opportunity to *start* attracting more customers to your business and then work on keeping them. Your customers will take notice when you do what others are unwilling to do to solve their problem and create a great experience.

Chapter 10 Notes

1   Bob Lederer, "How did Super Jets really feel about Joe's boast?" *Daily News*, September 12, 2018.

2   "Wyoming coach apologizes for flipping bird during Utah game," *Associated Press*, November 12, 2007.

3   Dan Gilbert, "Open Letter to Fans from Cavaliers Majority Owner Dan Gilbert," posted on the Cleveland Cavaliers website (since removed), July 8, 2010.

4   Tim Graham, "Rex Ryan guarantees Jets Super Bowl win," *ESPN*, February 24, 2011.

5   Mike Mazzeo, "Rex Ryan done making guarantees," *ESPN*, September 7, 2011.

6   Jake Trotter, "OU women's basketball: Courtney sticking by guarantee," *The Oklahoman*, March 8, 2009.

7   "OU AD says Paris has given enough," *Associated Press*, April 7, 2009.

8   R.B. Fallstrom, "Louisville reaches first title game," *The Spokesman-Review*, April 6, 2009.

9   "OU AD says Paris has given enough," *Associated Press*, April 7, 2009.

10 Vin A. Cherwood, "Courtney Paris to create community fund to pay back debt," *Tahoe Daily Tribune*, April 10, 2009.

INDEX

Made in the USA
Monee, IL
03 April 2021